BEEN THERE, DONE THAT

BEEN THERE, DONE THAT

RODNEY HUI

OM
publishing

First published 2000 by OM Publishing

06 05 04 03 02 01 00   7 6 5 4 3 2 1

OM Publishing is an imprint of Paternoster Publishing,
PO Box 300, Carlisle, Cumbria CA3 0QS, UK
and Paternoster Publishing USA
Box 1047, Waynesboro, GA 30830–2047

www.paternoster-publishing.com

British Library Cataloguing-in-Publication Data

A catalogue record for this book is available from the British Library

ISBN 1–85078–368–3

Cover design by Campsie
Typeset by Waverley Typesetters, Galashiels
Printed in Great Britain by
Cox & Wyman Limited, Reading

To KPC, my church, whose support and
help are an inspiration, and

To my wife, Irene, and our children,
Justin and Marianne,
who touch my life every day
and Jeanette, my ever-helpful sister

Contents

Contents

Preface

God's Uncanny Habit

Why this book?

Why not?

I have many reasons for not writing. Firstly, I am not a theologian. My formal studies in biblical knowledge are limited to a one-year course in Tasmania in 1985 and regular reading. This does not qualify me to be a theologian. I am told that one should hold academic degrees to earn that coveted label.

Secondly, there are already many similar books on the real life experiences of Christians. Most, if not all, will be far superior to this attempt of mine. My duplication may be surplus to requirements.

Thirdly, I know of many colleagues who have been in Operation Mobilisation[1] for many years who have far better tales to tell. Indeed, I fear I might have unknowingly replicated some of them here!

Lastly, I know of only two other people who have attempted to document events taking place in and around OM. I hope I have not rushed into an area where angels fear to tread.

Now for my reasons for writing. If I am so convinced of my own inadequacies, why am I determined to proceed?

To begin with, writing my own book has been a long-cherished dream. Some years back, I said in a candid interview in my church newsletter that my wish was to write a publication of some relevance. This product is the realisation of that dream.

Nonetheless, the real motivation in putting pen to paper came from several quarters. Rev David Wong, a friend and seasoned writer, lamented the dearth of Asian Christian authors when I last met him in India. He proceeded to challenge me to write something, telling of my experiences serving in OM. That was the start I needed.

Just to make sure I was on the right path with the right intentions, I asked Peter Maiden, the Associate International Director of OM (i.e. my boss) what he thought. He too encouraged me to embark on the journey, via a very down-to-earth line of questioning. His major concern was whether I had a willing publisher. I started hunting for one.

Then there was encouragement from friends and church-mates such as Lawrence Hee and Dr Goh Wei Leong, who have heard some of my anecdotes in my sermons. They suggested that I commit my experiences to print.

So here I am at the start of an interesting journey. At the point of writing, I have absolutely no idea when I will finish, or whether I will find a publisher.

I have requested the help of Sunny Goh, an established journalist with the knack of writing and a sharp eye for detail, to improve on my raw copy. I have a tendency to slip into Singlish (Singapore-brand English), and though this colourful form is more obvious when heard than read, I was pretty convinced of my ability to confuse my usage as well as my readers. I am indebted to Sunny.

Another person who gave my uncharted journey a kick-start is Rev Kenneth Boullier, vicar of an Anglican Church in Bristol, England. How does someone living so far north have so much to offer this book from the tropics? I can think of two reasons. One, Ken was the leader of an overland team I was involved with. He has kindly agreed to verify (and ahem, sanctify) the section on that particular rough trip. Two, he was the mentor who had a direct hand in introducing me to the basics of leading a team. He did a marvellous job and I remain his enthusiastic pupil.

So if you do not like what you read, send me the brickbats. If you enjoy it, these 'partners-in-print' deserve the bouquets far more than I do.

Finally, let me come to the most important reason that fires my determination. I embark on this writing mission in the hope that readers will discover that the Christian life, seemingly drab and dreary to the faint-hearted, is in fact liveable, practicable and workable to the warm-hearted.

As someone whose life revolves around missions and missionaries, I want readers to come away with the belief that God works in mundane as well as mysterious ways. He has an uncanny habit of working through average and ordinary people. The ordinary can become extraordinary when God works through us.

When you have finished walking this journey with me, I hope it can mark the start of your own journey. Tell me if you like it. Tell me if you don't. And tell me you must, if something along the way stirred or disturbed you.

In anticipation,

Rodney Hui
68, Lorong 16, Geylang
Association Building, #03-06
Singapore 398889
Email: rodhui@pacific.net.sg

---

[1] Operation Mobilisation is an international mission that seeks to share the love of Jesus Christ in many and varied ways. Readers are likely to be familiar with the ships *Logos II* and *Doulos* that OM operates.

Foreword

How can such a young man pack so much into life? As you read through the experiences Rodney has enjoyed – and sometimes endured – you will learn, you will laugh, at times you may cry. But most certainly, you will be challenged.

This is a book about life and about Christian ministry as it really is. The ups and the downs, the strengths of people and their weaknesses. The longer I am in Christian ministry the more I am amazed at the great variety of people whom God can use in quite extraordinary ways. I believe that as you read this book, you may begin to get a new vision of what God might do in and through you.

You will also be introduced to some of the most desperate parts of the world as far as the progress of the Gospel is concerned. I trust that many will be challenged to pray and to give. Some may even be challenged to be ambassadors for the Lord in these unreached parts of the world.

Thank you Rodney for an interesting, exciting, honest and challenging review of many of your experiences.

I see this book as Part One of Rodney's inspiring journey. I'm eagerly awaiting Part Two as I'm sure God has many more experiences ahead for him from which he will learn and as he writes them down for us, through which we will learn from these close encounters.

PETER MAIDEN
Associate International Co-ordinator
Operation Mobilisation

Chapter One

Four Dead, Two Alive

*'I tell you the truth, unless a kernel of
wheat falls to the ground and dies, it
remains only a single seed. But if it dies,
it produces many seeds.'*
John 12:24

It was Christmas 1974. David Adeney, OMF
missions spokesman, then Dean of the Discipleship Training Centre, Singapore, was speaking
at my church.

David, a supporter and advocate of Operation
Mobilisation in the early years, told us about a
group of OMers, all young people, who had been
involved in a fatal accident in Yugoslavia while
travelling overland from India to Europe.

Of the six in the Volkswagen van, four died.
(One year later, on the MV *Logos*, the training
ship OM operated, I had the joy and privilege
of working with one of the two survivors. Two
years later I was bound for travel on the same

highway in Yugoslavia where the accident took place.)

The tragic news moved me. I was saddened at the waste of young lives. But I was touched more deeply by the commitment and sacrifice of these young people. At the end of David's message, I made up my mind to dedicate my life to God like these young people who had given up their all in the name of divine service. Call it youthful romanticism or foolhardy idealism, but I was serious about the business of serving God. The only problem was I did not know how. But I was soon to find out.

Two months before David's message I had begun thinking about my future. I was coming to the end of my period of National Service and new plans had to be made. I had applied to study transportation at a university in Toronto, Canada, where my elder brother, Roger, was working.

If all went well I would begin the course in late 1975. I was looking forward to this exciting next step and so were other members of my family. Furthering one's education was a positive, albeit predictable, step towards a decent career. My student visa was being processed and the rest was to be a matter of time.

Except for one nagging thought.

The desire to serve the Lord kept popping up. It was gnawing at me, making me feel guilty and glad at the same time. The more I thought about it the more I wondered if God had dropped me a heavy hint through David. But how would God speak His mind? And when He did would I recognise it or mistake my wilfulness for His will?

Never once had I imagined that when I became a Christian I would become a missionary as well. I thought that only Westerners with a determined streak could fill such a role. My own experience of salvation began on the morning my mother died, in 1971. Her death made me wrestle with the question of where my mother was headed for. After turning this over and over in my mind, I was jolted by the realisation that I did not even know where I myself was headed for! Where would I end up if I had died there and then? If Christians were right about their faith, there would only be one of two destinations – heaven or hell.

Jennifer, my second sister, was a committed Christian. I had watched her life and had seen her upright testimony. I liked what I saw and I wanted that kind of life. That night, whether I was literally scared right out of hell or not, I told Jennifer I wanted to be a Christian. The Sunday after my mother's funeral I was in church.

Years later, Ajith Fernando, National Director of Youth for Christ, Sri Lanka, said that while most people come to Christ to meet a personal need, they stay with Christ because they know the Gospel is true. Ajith described my experience perfectly.

Today, when a Christian wants to serve the Lord in missions they inevitably invite challenges. There are questions about one's qualifications – educationally, spiritually, theologically, emotionally and vocationally (heavy stuff for a young adult) which have to be faced. Testimonies by missionaries almost always contain an element of struggle over these issues. Sometimes I get the impression that in order to serve God, one needs to be a super-being – i.e. super-spiritual, super-qualified, super-something or other. Like Jacob in the Old Testament such a person prevails after undergoing an emotion-drenching encounter with God. God finally gets a hold of them at the end of a tough wrestling match.

For me the questions were mercifully uncomplicated but there were still problems. Experienced Asian missionaries were a rarity so I never had an opportunity to consult even one about my serious interest in missions. Neither did I talk to anyone else.

My logic was simple – I had just given two years of National Service to my country, so why not give a similar term to the Lord? It seemed the most sensible thing to do. I would commit for two years for a start and then see how the Lord would lead me from there. To be honest, I was not even thinking of my grand life-plan beyond this timeframe. I intended to take one step at a time, and I was looking forward to the first step.

The news about the accident – four dead, two alive – was the nudge that I needed.

As it turned out, the two years have stretched to 24, and, God willing, I am still counting.

To say that the past 24 years have been the most exciting in my life is an understatement. Serving God is excitement itself! I get the feeling that some Christians regard serving God as boring. They look at pastors and missionaries and categorise them as some of the most uninteresting people around. Our drab wardrobe confirms that we are either from another era or another planet! Listening to us preach is a sure route to being lulled to sleep. If people who serve God are branded as boring, surely God must be boring too? Let me tell you that nothing is further from the truth – God is anything but a bore.

My time serving God has thus far involved me joining the MV *Logos* as a trainee. It has seen me travelling overland from Holland to Malaysia recruiting partners to back plans for a second ship, the MV *Doulos* which took to the seas a year later. I have lived in Malaysia, before moving on to Bangladesh where I assisted Mike Lyth, the OM leader, and became the fastest cyclist in Dhaka, overtaking all rickshaws on my daily runs to the bank. The next stop was India where I spent several months before rejoining the MV *Logos*.

I am not saying that life is totally without monotony, but even in monotony, good things can be found. Howard Peskett, former Dean of the Discipleship Training Centre, Singapore, once told me that there was such a thing as 'holy monotony'. Monotony may at times be some- thing we have to endure but holiness can be the fruit if we are willing to work at life.

On my next 'tour of duty' on the ship in 1978 in Okinawa, Japan, I received a telephone call from George Miley, then Director for the two ships MVs *Logos* and *Doulos*, to return to Singapore to take over the running of the *Logos* office from Frankie Low and Dr Allan Adams. At that time the work of OM was known only by the MV *Logos*.

My volunteer spirit was still fresh and without a second thought I answered yes. The prospect of running an office might, again, sound like boring work. It was far from being so.

From 1978 to 1988, I found myself living in Singapore, heading up the work of OM. During my tenure literally hundreds of Singaporeans and Malaysians were recruited for missions in OM. At the start we were one of a few agencies responsible for recruiting short-term mission- aries. We found a readiness among young people to commit themselves to a short-term stint. These volunteers would have been lost had we insisted on a long-term contract. By the hundreds they came. Many eventually returned to their home countries and even today a high percentage of them are still involved in long-term missions and/or church work.

Yet, it was not always that way. In the early days we were considered 'new kids on the block' in mission circles. Criticisms were levelled at OM. Perhaps it was my fault, at the tender age of 24, I could not help looking young and inexperienced! We were accused of poaching young people, we were criticised for our inexperience, for the many mistakes we made and the blunders we committed.

Through the years thankfully, people began to accept the fact that we have grown in maturity, experience, responsibility and accountability. After a quarter of a century of our ministry we enjoy a high degree of goodwill and credibility in all the countries where we have established a presence. How things have changed!

As the workload multiplied, it also expanded geographically. Acting for Dr Adams much of the time, I was able to help establish the work of OM in other parts of East Asia. New offices were opened and soon we were riding the crest of an on-rushing wave in our recruiting efforts. The timing was perfect for East Asians to go out in missions, and OM 'happened' to be in the right place, at the right time to provide the avenues for service. From Korea, Hong Kong, the Philippines, Malaysia, Singapore, Indonesia, Papua New Guinea, Australia and New Zealand, they all came.

At first they had heard only about the MV *Logos*, but the ship soon ran out of space. In

1976 we crossed the threshold by opening up the rest of OM. In the next two decades several thousand served with OM in various parts of the world – in Europe, North Africa, the Middle East, South and Central Asia, India, and, of course, on the two ships. In addition, several hundreds more each year would participate in our short-term evangelistic campaigns. Presently, more than six hundred people from East Asia and the Pacific are serving in and around OM, amounting to approximately 15 per cent of our worldwide work force.

Marital bliss came in 1985. Irene, a university graduate with social work experience, joined OM in 1980 to work among immigrants in Britain. The following year she moved to Pakistan where she led a women's team (besides driving the team van). I figured that a lady who survived driving for a year in Pakistan without a scratch on the vehicle, much less an accident, was worthy of the greatest respect! In her third year I invited her to be my bookkeeper, with no knowledge at that point that she would eventually become my life partner. Working together in the office afforded us much time together. It became a foundation in understanding our roles in OM in our matrimonial years.

Following our marriage we took a sabbatical year away from OM to study at the Missionary Training College in Tasmania, Australia, run by Worldwide Evangelisation for Christ. It was an enjoyable and memorable year for us. We spent a lot of time buried in books and assignments. As far as practical duties were concerned I became the official grasscutter and part-time farmer on campus. This was a big deal for a city-dweller. One does not often get to see cows, much less milk them, in urban Singapore. Although I did not make big money, this was a voluntary job, I did end up holding the proud record of milking cows for six months in college!

When milk supply exceeded demand during college holidays, I would whip up some fresh cream from the milk to eat with freshly-picked strawberries. Irene and I ended up putting on kilos! We are now convinced that there is much to milk from theological study.

On our return to Singapore I took responsibility for OM in South-East Asia. Justin, our son, was born in 1988. As a family we spent several months on the MV *Doulos* sailing around the region.

In 1990 we moved to Hong Kong. The purpose was to establish the work of OM in the territory as a springboard into China, Central Asia and Mongolia. The people whom God had already raised and put in place before our arrival made this job easy. Today, this part of the ministry, though small in size, is in fact quite significant in purpose.

Marianne, our daughter, was 'made in Hong Kong'. Our Hong Kong friends used to tell us that with a son and a daughter, we were a perfect family. Whilst we know that we are far from perfect we do immensely enjoy our family life.

In 1992 Dr Allan Adams, with others in major leadership, appointed me as the Associate Area Co-ordinator of OM East Asia Pacific. In January 1995 Allan effectively passed the baton to me. Due to the nature of my new role, which involved much travel, we made the decision to return to Singapore.

This book would not be complete, and my life would not be where it is today, if it were not for several people who have given so much to enrich my life. Whatever character formation that has taken place in my life, apart from God through His beloved Son Jesus Christ, whom I am totally committed to, I owe it to three people – George Verwer, George Miley and Allan Adams. I am ever thankful to God and to these men for the indelible mark they have left on my life.

Another group of people who have meant a lot to me are my immediate colleagues whom I have always considered friends – Peter Maiden, Dale Rhoton, Bernd Gulker, Joseph D'Souza, Francois Vosloo, Joop Strietmann, Dennis Wright, Tony Kirk, Dave Hicks, Duanne Grasman and Mike Wakely. They have not ceased to show patience and esteem to someone who is always five or ten minutes late in contributing to a discussion of global magnitude! If you are able to detect any snatches of insight or wisdom in this book it is probably due to their influence.

Last but by no means least are the staff of OM Singapore who have accepted me for what I am and allowed me to get away with many silly things. It has been said that unless one quarrels and argues one never learns how to resolve conflicts. But I beg to differ in the case of my relationship with Kenneth Bong, OM Singapore Director. Since 1987 we have worked together and never had a heated exchange, let alone a serious quarrel. That I believe is a special privilege I enjoy and continue to appreciate. It is simply God's grace at work in two people who are quite different in their make up. Such relationships are precious and take effort to build.

This then is a synopsis of my 24 years in missions. In the ensuing chapters you will read of some of my experiences and encounters.

Even as king, David never forgot his humble roots. I am not of course royalty but I do like to return, periodically, to the day when I made that commitment to serve God. I owe my life in missions to many people, but I owe it most to those four young people killed in the traffic accident in Yugoslavia whom I never met, never knew.

Chapter Two

Sail On, Sailor

> *'. . . make every effort to add to your faith
> goodness; and to goodness, knowledge; and to
> knowledge, self-control; and to self-control,
> perseverance; and to perseverance, godliness; and
> to godliness, brotherly kindness; and to brotherly
> kindness, love.'*
> 2 Peter 1:5–7

Look out world, here I come. I am going to turn you upside down!

That was my intention as I joined the MV *Logos* in April 1975. I did not dare verbalise my goal for fear of being accused of boasting. But wasn't that what the brave disciples in the Book of Acts did in their own world? If they could do it, I was ready to give it a try in mine.

I was young, only twenty. Looking at young people today, I can understand their idealism. I was like that once. Indeed, I was not only an idealist; I was a legalist as well. Any Christian with some years behind them will tell you that this is a deadly combination!

My youthful pride didn't last long though. No sooner had I stepped on board the ship than God, with His usual sense of humour, brought me down to earthy reality with a bump.

After an hour of orientation about life on board, 13 of us, all men mainly from East and West Malaysia and Singapore, were directed to the bow where we would find our accommodation. Images of a luxury liner floated through our minds – portholes with seaviews, beds with clean sheets, en-suite bathroom and toilet. In blissful ignorance we walked along the alleyway towards our accommodation, we failed to detect the conciliatory (or was it comforting?) tone of Mike Stachura, the Programme Director, when he assured us that the accommodation 'wasn't too bad'. We took his word for it. We were simple, gullible, rookie missionaries, humble servants of God, ready to believe anything! As it turned out Mike was guilty of a gross under-statement.

The dormitory was located at the very front part of the ship. We squeezed through the door-way to view our bunks. They were stacked three levels high with little space in between and definitely insufficient room for one to sit up in bed! The dormitory looked and smelled like a dungeon. We were told that it was in fact a dumping ground for everyone else's luggage.

As trainees we were supposed to be uncomplaining. It was after all unspiritual to complain and we didn't want the ship family to learn that the first thing the new trainees had done was find fault with their accommodation. It would be dishonest to say that we were not disappointed though. We decided to have a thorough clean up in order to make our quarters fit for living in. All 13 of us quickly set to work and within a day the dormitory was completely transformed. We felt like proud occupants of a new house.

There was something else we were not told. Nobody warned us about the anchor chain locker located directly beneath the dormitory, or told us that the two round pillars in the middle of our cabin housed the twin anchor chains. When we arrived at our first port in Kuching, Sarawak, we experienced what it sounded and felt like when the two 2-tonne anchors were dropped into the sea.

We were all sound asleep when it happened. Thud! An earth-shattering roar thundered in our cabin. It sounded like a bomb had exploded. Adrenaline was pumping, we jumped up from our bunks, crashing our heads on the bunks above us. Only when we dashed out of our cabin to find out what had happened and to determine the damage were we informed about the anchor chains. Other ship members collapsed with laughter when they heard about our reaction.

After this introduction we learned fast. We made sure that we were either absent when the anchor was dropped, or would find out the time the officer would drop anchor. After a few more occurrences of this 'surround sound' (we had it 15 years ahead of Hollywood technosound!), we learned to anticipate it by the initial clang when metal struck metal. We would then bury our heads in our pillows if we could not get out in time. However, to get our own back, we would withhold this information from any visitor, until it was too late for them!

Life at sea was anything but routine in those early years. There was always much to do. The ship was organised in departments – steward, engine, deck, training, galley, programme and the book exhibition.

On the present ships, MV *Doulos* and MV *Logos II*, the book exhibitions have permanent roofs and lifts so that books can be transferred easily from the book-holds to the relevant deck. On the old MV *Logos* however the book exhibition was housed in an old-fashioned tarpaulin tent, which had to be erected and taken down when we pulled in and out of a port. In addition, the entire exhibition of books had to be packed in containers to be loaded into the holds, only to be taken out again when we reached the next port. It was time-consuming and hard work, but few complained.

Community life at sea had its rules and regulations. In addition to the Merchant Navy safety requirements, the ship had its own policies and practices. Some of them would be classified quaint, if not from another age or planet. For instance, customs officers found it hard to believe that the *Logos* was a 'dry' ship – no liquor was allowed on board.

Regular ships with regular seamen are prime targets for the flesh trade. Some ports are notorious for their red-light activities. MV *Logos* was probably the only vessel in the world at that time that was an exception. We were different but those in the flesh trade did not know that. There had been 'ladies' who boarded the ship to offer their services. Imagine the embarrassment for one brother when he returned to his cabin to find a 'lady' waiting, she was promptly shown the way out!

To avoid 'the appearance of evil' and to maintain the sanctity of a Christian community, there were strict rules governing behaviour between the sexes on the ship. For instance, a male and a female crew or staff member were not allowed to engage in long conversations alone. If you had to leave the ship for an errand the rule was to go out with someone of the same sex. This also served as a security measure. In some ports there were incidents of mugging and the ship authorities would insist that members go out in groups.

What if there was a particular girl you found yourself attracted to? What if you wanted to develop a friendship with her? Well you could not, unless the two of you had completed a year on the ship or in OM. If this was the case then you could talk to one of the ship leaders. If a ship leader was in favour he would approach the girl. If the girl was attached, the ship leader would inform you and thus save you the embarrassment of approaching her directly. But if it turned out that she also had an interest in you, then both of you would be given Social Permission (SP).

SP allowed the two of you to meet and talk and develop your friendship. SP would be made known publicly to the ship family to avoid misunderstanding should you be seen together. Often when SP was announced, normally over mealtime, there would be banging of cutlery and catcalls – to the amusement and delight of the ship family. In due course some relationships developed into courtship and eventually marriage. For this, couples would go home. Others discovered that they were not compatible and their relationships died a natural death.

Through the years this policy has not changed much. It is still enforced today in a more modified fashion. The reason for the requirement of completing one year before recruits can ask for SP is to encourage new recruits to give their undivided attention to training and learning in the first year. It also prevents immature and premature relationships that do not last. Without such distractions, or entanglements, in the first year new recruits can concentrate on service. It is also a good opportunity for new recruits, especially the younger ones, to learn to wait upon the Lord in this important aspect of life.

The funniest story about SP on the ship happened many years ago. One fellow came to the Director's office to request SP with a particular girl. Whilst it was not inappropriate for him to make this request the Director was concerned that this fellow was absolutely convinced that this was the girl God had spoken to him about. (Of course all of us have a tendency to spiritualise our desire and interest – attributing it to God's will when in actual fact it is our own fancy.) The Director advised him to wait and pray about it for a week or two. He accepted the counsel and left the office.

Shortly afterwards there was another knock on the door and in walked another young man asking for SP with the same girl. The Director was wondering what conviction this young man would claim. He claimed that God had spoken to him through His Word.

The story did not end there. Lo and behold, a third man came to see the Director, asking for SP with the same girl! You can imagine the confusion the girl would have felt had these three men approached her directly! Needless to say the Director promptly put an end to this episode – he did not give in to the wishes of any of the three young men.

Within the ship community the dress code was modest. However, it was difficult to fix upon a dress code that was acceptable to all cultures represented on board. What resulted was a gradual evolution of the *Logos* fashion! Ship ladies wore trousers (because of the steep stairs on board) with a sleeved blouse (bare arms were considered immodest) covering the elbows. I laugh just picturing it now but it was *the* fashion of the day! Jeans, especially the skin-hugging ones, were disallowed for the ladies as they were classified offensive to men. Today, thankfully, you will find ladies wearing jeans on board.

The men all inevitably wore kurtas, picked up from India, complete with Indian sandals and an Indian shoulder bag for tracts. These became the trademarks of men's missionary fashion on board *Logos*! Up until recently a Singaporean pastor was still complaining about a *Logos* team who came to his church in the 1970s in flip-flops and kurtas!

Another peculiarity (so it seems now), was the no-camera policy. This was to avoid us looking like camera-toting tourists. If a person had a camera it had to be used discreetly. For this reason my collection of pictures from the 1970s is meagre. Thankfully we have left this policy behind many years ago.

It would not be right if I did not mention the small matter of seasickness, which is dreaded by many. A sufferer is sick not once, but all the time. The only thing to do is to do nothing. Even doing nothing, such as lying in bed, does not help. Some would say that this is the worst thing to do.

When seasickness goes on for days on a voyage it can be depressing. Just when you feel the worst you will inevitably come across those who never get sick telling you your sickness is 'all in the mind'. I know of many who never had victory in this sickness no matter how hard they had prayed. It is nothing spiritual. Some people are just prone to it while others simply are not troubled. Thankfully I belonged to the latter group.

One comical incident took place in a port in Asia. On the night before the ship sailed the Captain informed the ship community that it would leave the berth at 6.00 am the next day. One of the Indian men on board who was prone to seasickness was not looking forward to the voyage. As we approached departure time he was already complaining about giddiness and nausea. At 6.30 am he could bear it no longer; he dashed out of his cabin, up the stairs and out on deck. He leaned over the gunwale to throw up into the sea, only to realise that we were still alongside the berth. There was a delay in departure but the Captain had not informed us. We hoped that no unfortunate passer-by had been hit with this shower of vomit!

I have ridden out at least half a dozen typhoons in very choppy seas and threatening conditions. One time several of us were working on deck when suddenly the ship hit a trough in the Mediterranean Sea. The aft slammed into the water and before we knew it the deck was awash with the cold Mediterranean Sea water. Had we not clung on to the railings, we would have been swept overboard.

Another time we were in the Bay of Bengal when we received a typhoon warning. The ship rode out the typhoon, resulting in the delay of our arrival in Chittagong, Bangladesh.

At other times, when the sea was calm, I enjoyed doing painting work on one of the masts, like I did when we were in the North Seas with the cold wind blowing. Those were carefree and precious moments. Now and then we were rewarded by the sight of dolphins swimming alongside or at the bow of the ship.

Budget was tight in the early years. When gifts in kind were forthcoming they were welcomed unreservedly. When I first boarded the ship received from the Carnation company a donation of a container of 'Spreadables'. These were cans of tuna fish in mayonnaise which spread easily on bread, and tasted good – at first.

Once we had eaten 'Spreadables' for the next few months however, as main or supplementary course, entrée or finger food, the flavour faded. We began to feel like the Israelites in their experience with manna in the wilderness – we were sick of it. And yes, our attitude soon became like that of the Israelites too. It was little wonder that after a while, we did not mind being invited out for local food. Anything to break the pattern! Being invited out by local believers was always a treat, especially for the bachelors who had little else to eat (the ladies at least could bake!). It was such a delight, for instance, when we were in Cebu. A Chinese church brought two roast pigs, baskets of mangoes and an unlimited supply of Coca Cola for the ship family. It was a happy day of feasting for everyone!

Since then the ship ministry has come a long way in the area of food. It is true – food does affect morale! It is not being unspiritual to eat proper and sufficient food. We are not as frugal as we used to be. Proper planning has improved both menu and diet.

As trainees we often joined teams to work with churches and missionaries onshore. I found myself on a team up river in Limbang, Sarawak. In Kobe I was stranded with a land team while the ship rode out a typhoon. In Macau I was part of a large *Logos* team engaged in an evangelistic campaign (17 years later, working from Hong Kong, I was able to send more teams to the same churches).

Of my many team experiences I will never forget one in the Philippines. The ship was berthed in Bacolod and I was part of a team of five men told to carry out a week-long pro-gramme in Dumaguate, approximately 200 kilometres south. For this purpose we were given the use of a ship van. As an afterthought, the Programme Manager gave us 300,000 calendar tracts instructing us to distribute all of them before returning. There were 30 boxes in all.

We thought this not only impossible, but also downright ridiculous even to attempt in a week. But my team leader, S. N. Das, from India, was not perturbed. Stories of mass literature distribution by OM in India were legendary and S. N. Das calmly accepted the assignment.

When we had loaded all the boxes, there was not much space left for people, let alone luggage. We had to sit on top of the luggage and boxes.

Gerit, from Canada, and S. N. Das, both veterans in mass literature distribution, came up with a simple strategy. To avoid duplicating our distribution we would drive one route to Dumaguate and return by another. There were many towns and villages along the route. As soon as people were spotted ahead, Gerit, as driver, would sound the horn to attract attention while the rest of us would get ready with stacks of the calendar tracts (good for a year!) in our hands. Then we let fly! Invariably people would stoop to pick them up. I have good reason to suspect that this is one method of leaflet distribution used in India!

Halfway to Dumaguate we were descending a hill on a gravel road where below farmers were harvesting sugar cane. As we rounded a bend we were enveloped by smoke from burning sugar cane. A truck loomed in front of our windscreen, swerved, missed us by inches, and plummeted down the ravine. Moments before we had seen a woman walking by the roadside. She was no longer there. The truck had hit her, throwing her into the ravine.

We stopped our Ford Transit and jumped out to check the situation. Looking down we saw the overturned truck with two bodies lying close by. I ran down to see if I could help. I checked the pulse of the driver. Nothing, he was dead. I went to the woman. Half her scalp was ripped open. I also noticed she was pregnant. I felt for her pulse, but she too was dead. S. N. Das shouted to our team, 'Let's get out of here!' He must have seen something we had not.

As we drove away a stricken-looking boy begged to travel with us. He did not speak any English. It dawned upon us that he was the companion of the driver. We drove for about 10 km to the nearest town and reported the incident to the police there. As our van was undamaged they correctly assumed that we were neither involved in nor had caused the accident. In fact it was caused entirely by the truck driver who was driving on the wrong side of the road. A police officer returned with us to the scene of the accident.

By now a crowd had gathered and they were angry, brandishing knives and sickles. The police officer fired a shot into the air. This stopped everyone in their tracks. As we had done our part we left to continue on our way.

That night I couldn't sleep. I was troubled with doubts about my salvation. That afternoon had been the first time I had witnessed sudden death. What would have happened to me had I died that day? Where would I be? Though I had volunteered to serve the Lord I was still a young Christian then.

In my restlessness I turned to the Bible and was led to Galatians 2:20 – 'I am crucified with Christ'. This statement resounded in my mind and heart throughout the night. Like Paul, I began to realise that the life I lived was no longer mine. It belonged and still belongs to Jesus. This verse was a real gift from the Lord in my time of need. It still has a life-changing effect on me now and then when I have the occasion to return to it.

This was the beginning of a lifelong habit – returning to the Word of God for assurance and comfort whenever I am confronted with pressure and temptations. This habit has proved to be a life-saver.

The Rodney who returned to the ship after that week away was a very different Rodney from the one who left it. Praise God indeed for His mercy.

Having set out with the intention of turning the world upside down, at the end of five months I found my own world turned upside down and inside out. My idealism quickly gave way to realism. My pat answers to the world's problems were painfully inadequate.

I joined the ship with a lot of ideas about what true Christian life should be. My ideas were mistaken. Perhaps as a result of my upbringing, or perhaps from a brand of 'churchianity' that fed a legalistic streak, my world was a dichotomous black and white. I judged other churches, denominations, evangelists, authors and writers in monotones, never in colour or shades. I even judged Christians by the Bible they read. It must be the King James Version because I knew of no better version.

As I stepped out of my comfort zone into the world to serve the Lord I was uncomfortable. I found out very quickly that my neat and tidy theories did not apply to all people and all situations. I embarked on a course to unlearn some of the baggage I had picked up. The MV *Logos*, in God's grace, was a fertile learning ground for me.

On board were people from 30 nations, all from different denominational backgrounds. It was a pleasant surprise to find that they were not so bad. In fact they were good people. I liked and enjoyed what I saw. I was impressed by the godliness of the Indians and the resourcefulness of the Europeans. I discovered that another brand of music, different from the one I was used to, was quite acceptable, and really, what you wore was not as important as what you were in your heart.

I even became unstuck from the King James Version (Shakespearean English had always been a problem for me in school anyway!), the only Bible allowed in my church. I plucked up the courage to read other, simpler versions in English. Lightning did not strike me dead and for the first time in my life I revelled in reading God's Word and found that I could truly understand it!

Another significant lesson learned in my early years with OM was about prayer and praying. We had prayer meetings every Friday night starting at 8.00 pm and ending at 2.00 am. It was my habit to rise at 6.00 am for my devotion. How I survived those years I will never know, except by God's grace I believe. But sleep could be sacrificed if prayer made a difference to the world. We prayed for anything and everything, for people and for countries. It was in these prayer meetings that I learned about the spiritual condition and the needs of the world. I believe the knowledge and information I received at this time helped in strengthening my commitment to world missions. I believe it changed the course of my life for God, and for good.

Let me end this chapter by saying that I am a firm believer in the ship ministry. Unfortunately the *Logos* ran aground in 1988 at the southern tip of Latin America. She was succeeded by a third ship, renamed the MV *Logos II*. It was liberating to discover God in a fresh way through relationships and evangelism. The exposure to the virtues of love, discipline, sacrifice and esteeming others better than oneself in a close-knit community laid in me a foundation that still stands me in good stead as I relate to all kinds of people today. I have no hesitation in encouraging young people to do a stint on one of the OM ships.

Chapter Three

Going for a Song

*'But seek first his kingdom and his righteousness,
and all these things will be given to you as well.'*
Matthew 6:33

*'And this gospel of the kingdom will be preached
in the whole world as a testimony to all nations,
and then the end will come.'*
Matthew 24:14

People often ask me what serving the Lord is like.

Besides telling them that it is absorbing I add that serving God has to do with our attitude. We can make it as pleasant, adventurous and interesting as we want it to be, or we can let it be unpleasant, boring and frustrating. It is all a matter of attitude. I learned this early in my life when I left home and country. Paul's motto in 1 Corinthians 9:22b 'I have become all things to all men . . .' was a slogan of inspiration as I started out sharing Jesus with both Christians

and non-Christians. It has helped me survive all
these years.

Often the perception is that once we have made
the decision to serve God we are in for a life of
hardship, suffering, sacrifice and little else.
Perhaps we have picked this idea up from books,
biographies and sermons. I know that at times I
have been guilty of conveying this idea. Of course
serving God does involve hardship and sacrifice;
I have had the joy of knowing many of God's
servants who had suffered and sacrificed much.
But there is also a tremendous sense of joy and
fulfilment when we know we are doing God's
will. Often we choose only to hear of the diffi-
culties rather than the joy of serving Jesus.

In my case I can say that life has been remark-
ably adventurous, and the joy, immeasurable.
Joining OM and sailing on the MV *Logos* was
considered an odd course of action compared to
the paths taken by my peers. They were establishing their careers as I took to the sea. Recently,
after 23 years, my army mates got together for a
reunion. Almost all of us are family men now,
with steady jobs and established careers. As we
talked we were amazed at how fresh our
memories were of our two years together almost
a quarter of a century ago.

It was a surprise to me to hear their favourable
reactions to my work. They used words like
'worthwhile', 'meaningful', 'great work', to
describe what I was doing. Such responses from

non-Christians were I thought a wonderful testimony to God's favour and blessings.

Matthew 6:33, quoted at the beginning of this chapter, was the assurance I received from the Lord when I made the decision to serve Him. I do not believe that this is a decision one makes only once in a lifetime. I believe it is a conscious choice one makes consistently. Looking back, I can testify to God's faithfulness in my life every step of the way. As I have kept my side of the commitment, He has kept His promise. And I am still trusting Him and walking by faith.

Reviewing, or taking stock of my life, is an exercise I engage in every now and again. It is true that my life has taken a different direction than I had perhaps planned but the fringe benefits are enormous. I must stress however that these benefits, or blessings, come as a result of obedience, they are not the reason for obedience.

I must clarify too that when I say benefits I don't necessarily mean the material kind. More often than not blessings and benefits arrive in intangible forms. I have had the opportunity to travel so much I have exhausted several passports already. I have been exposed to many cultures and facets of life; worked with internationals and nationals; lived on ships and a riverboat; lived in five different countries; all in a span of a few short years. Such blessings are intangible.

In case this gives the impression that being involved with missions is all glory and comfort, let me assure you that this is not the case. OM's level of comfort in the earlier years was extremely basic. I have slept under all kinds of Spartan conditions whilst travelling – in classrooms, out under the stars, in freezing temperatures, in vans, in the back of OM trucks, on rooftops, in an Indian garage, in luggage compartments on trains and ferries, churches, homes, storerooms, on buses and lately on planes. The wear and tear of years of such a lifestyle will show on the body, although thankfully in my case the effects are minimal. I am aware of the occupational hazards that come with serving God but I still believe it is a privilege to do so!

My motivation is God's faithfulness in my life. I am also inspired by His love for the lost. I do not have an easy, natural talent for winning people to Christ, but I have always tried, many times unsuccessfully, to maintain that motivation of love for all people. My deepest desire is to see the Gospel advanced into the hearts of many. This motivation did not come overnight, it took time to nourish and nurture. If we are not careful, the cares of this world over-take us and before we know it, such motivation is elbowed out entirely.

I thought two years was the limit I would give to God. But His will was not mine, and His plans, not my fancy. Having learned so much on the initial stretch, I did not need any persuasion to extend my time with OM, how easy it was just to continue. In the mid-1970s the enterprise of Christian missions was at its pioneering stage, especially in the involvement of Asians. OM had only a few basic requirements – if your church gave their blessing and you had a heart for hard work and a love for Jesus, there would be a place for you.

So I signed on for a further year. This meant that my plans to study in Canada were shelved. At times I am tempted to imagine what I could have become had I not chosen to serve God. Maybe I could have been quite successful or even quite rich. But knowing the deceit in my own heart, I shudder at the prospect of living life without the Lord Jesus. I know I would not be strong or humble enough to handle success. How true it is when the Bible says that the road that leads to destruction is easy and many take it. I want to be found walking the straight and narrow road, just like many of my colleagues and friends who are trying to do so regardless of their profession and income. I firmly believe that God in His mercy will lead, guide and provide for those who live lives that please Him.

Let's return to some lessons learned in the early *Logos* years. Upon signing on I was assigned to the Deck Department. I had absolutely no idea what deck work was and my knowledge of the

Deck Department was zero, but I was willing to learn.

My fellow deckmen were Ser Kiat, a fellow Singaporean, Samuel Castro, who is now the Director of OM Mexico, Kristian Renling, a Swede, and Jans Dahlum, a nineteen-year-old Norwegian who was our bosun. What a fabulous time we had working together.

We were the muscle men of the ship. While life went on inside the ship we were out in the sun, rain and cold doing necessary maintenance work. We sweated and we froze, we pulled and pushed. We chipped, stripped paint and painted over what we had chipped. We must have painted the entire ship several times over! This was necessary as rust quickly accumulates when the environment is salty. We were so pleased with the way we kept the ship in shape that we did not mind the physical work. We just did all as 'unto the Lord'. It was a blissful year. It was also a crash course in learning about myself and about evangelism.

The hard work of painting provided me with an analogy I will always remember describing what God was doing in my life. When we saw rust coming through the bulkhead or deckhead of the ship we knew it was treatment time. This involved an arduous process. The first step was to chip off the rust. This was the dirtiest part of the process but the most important as if the rust was not thoroughly chipped out the layers of paint would only be cosmetic, the metal would quickly rust through again.

Chipping got rid of the root problem. To do it correctly we had to put on a pair of goggles, our overalls, safety shoes and a cap. Then we would hammer away. Once done we washed the 'wound'. Next, a layer of thinner was applied, followed by a coat of primer. If the rust was bad, an additional coat of primer was applied. The undercoat was next, before we applied the final coat of gleaming, shiny gloss, which literally transformed the metal to look as good as new. Samuel and I were working partners and we always ended our work with a deep sense of satisfaction.

I saw that process mirrored in my life. I saw the Lord patiently chipping away the dirty rust. This usually was a painful but necessary process. While some areas of my life were at the primer stage, other areas were still at the chipping phase. Even now I am convinced that the Lord is still transforming me. It can be quite discouraging when I see old rust appearing just when I thought I had overcome some personal faults. Praise God for His perseverance. I am learning to be patient with myself. More than that, I am also recognising God's work in others and learning to be patient with them too.

Everyone on board worked a regular eight-hour day, longer if their department was short-handed. The opportunities we had to share

Jesus were taken outside of our work hours. In this respect it was not unlike a church where members hold regular jobs. Because I could play the guitar fairly well I was often included in the onshore programmes – student meetings, youth meetings, church or open-air meetings. I had no training in public speaking or singing, I was thrown right in at the deep end! This was learning by doing – on-the-job training.

My first experience of public speaking took place in the Philippines when I joined the open-air team led by Ray Lenztsch, veteran open-air evangelist. Ray needed someone to provide the music and I seemed always to be available and willing. Music, or rather noise, is a good way of attracting a crowd in Asia. The team sang a popular ship tune and soon a crowd gathered. Ray began to speak. Having done my part I began to relax and eye the crowd. I would get some tracts ready and engage in some conversation when the session ended. Then I heard my name mentioned.

'And now we have Rodney from Singapore to share what God means to him,' I heard Ray saying. Before I knew what was happening, I was pushed forward to give my testimony. To this day I cannot remember what I mumbled!

Another time in Japan a Japanese man by the name of Akio acted as my interpreter. We thought we would have a go at preaching in public in a shopping arcade. We got hold of two stools and I stood on one and Akio stood on the other. I began in my Singlish, or rather broken English and Akio interpreted me. We went on for about fifteen minutes. I should have realised that the Japanese do not stop for anything, much less to listen to two odd fellows jabbering away. When we stopped I felt happy that I had given a good message. At least to me it had been good. To ensure that I had in fact done a good job I asked Akio what he thought of my preaching. He said, 'I didn't understand a single word you said, so I gave my own message in Japanese.'

In Korea the Programme Manager informed me that there was going to be a television programme featuring the *Logos*, and asked if I could get a small group together to sing for this. By this point I was living the motto of the ship and was ready for anything, anywhere, anytime. But this was different; we were appearing on television! We had to be good. I recruited Joy, from the USA and Margaret, from the UK, to form a trio. Having heard of Peter, Paul and Mary, the famous folk group, we wondered if this would launch Rodney, Joy and Margaret. Any fantasy of music contracts fizzled out very quickly, but we did sing on Korean television. And this was not the last time, other television opportunities were to follow.

While growing up in the 1960s I was introduced to all kinds of pop music. My brother was a leading member of a pop group and I attended their practice sessions held in our kitchen. It was not a privileged invitation – the noise and music attracted half of the boys in the street. After all they were using electric guitars and real drums! In the course of time I began to memorise lyrics from artistes like The Beatles, The Animals, The Rolling Stones, Cliff Richard, and so on. With this background, it is not difficult for me to understand the musical tastes of young people today.

When I first became a Christian I worried that my love of pop music was incompatible with my faith. I wasn't helped by the uncompromising stance which some Christians take on this issue. Now I enjoy all sorts of music and am not critical of others whose particular musical tastes differ from mine or who do not enjoy music at all. I am above all very glad that I can now appreciate the important place music can play in the church and evangelism.

It was with great anticipation that we awaited the arrival of Frank Fortunato in 1975, he was to join the ship at Istanbul. Frank was synonymous with OM music; we were already singing and using his songs. We knew of his gift in music but in reality he was even better than we had imagined. Frank was one of the two survivors of the Yugoslavia crash.

On board we were getting nervous as the Istanbul programme would feature for the first time, the *Logos* folk rock group, and a concert would be held in a public auditorium seating more than a thousand people. We were apprehensive because we knew that no such group existed!

The ship sailed into Istanbul. Originally we had planned to stay for a week only but on our way into the harbour the ship rammed into a ferry resulting in court hearings and an extended stay. Frank arrived a day after the ship, as the concert was scheduled for the following week he went to work without delay. He auditioned all ship members interested in taking part, deckmen, carpenters, cooks, pantry girls, office workers all gave it a try. At the end of the audition, 28 people were selected, out of which a core group of eight would be the 'real' singers.

Working out some basic choreography for the songs was a hilarious process. Non-artistic or non-dramatic people tend not to move in tempo but we had a good time practising in earnest. My good friend, Steve Wong from Hong Kong, a talented singer and guitarist, was the soloist and lead tenor. As there was no one to play bass guitar I volunteered. Up to this point I had never played the bass guitar but I was soon doing this on a regular basis.

The Istanbul concert was a resounding success. The auditorium was packed with people, all non-Christian and non-church-going folk. The *Logos* Singers were in business.

None of us had much singing ability in the beginning and all of us sang with different accents. We were not however lacking in enthusiasm. The *Logos* Singers became the main event and a crowd-puller in each port we visited, in the Mediterranean and Europe. We would start with some folk songs, followed by more serious numbers that contained Christian messages. We would perform before crowds of hundreds and thousands, in Egypt, Malta, Tunisia, Sicily, Italy, Palma, Spain, Portugal, Sweden, Belgium, Norway and the United Kingdom. Our biggest crowd was in Lisbon, Portugal, where an estimated 5,000 people came to watch us. This was a real testimony to the ability of Frank and a group of willing volunteer singers. The *Logos* Singers were the forerunner to today's International Night conducted by the *Logos II* and *Doulos* in many ports. Before the *Logos* Singers disbanded we recorded our songs and apparently thousands of tapes were sold.

Today I still play the guitar but I do not sing as much as I used to. I still have a deep desire to learn to communicate in a fresh way the marvellous saving grace of Jesus Christ. I don't think I will ever stop playing. Nor learning.

Chapter Four

Streaking Ahead

'Suppose one of you wants to build a tower.
Will he not first sit down and estimate the cost
to see if he has enough money to complete it?
For if he lays the foundation and is not able to
finish it, everyone who sees it will ridicule him,
saying, "This fellow began to build and was
not able to finish." '
Luke 14:28–30

One of the principles I have learned in OM is the principle of counting the cost – plan before you do, then finish the job.

This appears simple enough to put into practice. Being single and young when I started out with limited wealth and without commitments to tie me down, it was quite straightforward to count the cost, and even more so to forsake all for Christ, as there wasn't a lot to forsake in the first place! It was only when I started a family of my own that I discovered that the issues were more complex and harder to put into practice.

For all its simplicity embarking on the work of God can be complicated. Counting the cost in God's work involves the practical, tangible matter of money. The bottom line for many of our endeavours, apart from people, is finance. With sufficient funds and people we are able to execute our plans to completion. Without either we are destined for an early termination, even the risk of ridicule. Having one without the other is not enough. Both are necessary.

Having faith in God to move His people to give generously continues to be both a battle and a blessing. At home I had never trusted God for the provision of cash. As I embarked on missions I was exposed to this concept. We were taught to trust God for our own personal upkeep. Each person in OM was responsible for seeing their own needs met through prayer.

How we exercise faith, how one prays in God's will for God's provision and where work – that is, the aspect of budgeting, informing others and challenging people to give – comes into the picture are questions I am still pondering. I am certain however that living by faith is a principle of the Christian life.

The formation of a travelling team to spread the vision for a second OM ship gave me the opportunity to learn firsthand about faith, initiative, action and the volunteer spirit.

I was approaching the end of my time on the MV *Logos* and wondering what was next. Where was God leading me? Would He show me specifically or did I have to find out for myself? I did not spend too much time worrying, I had a feeling God already had His plans. Ken Boullier, an Englishman, provided the missing link I was waiting for.

Ken approached me one day and asked me if I would like to be part of a team he was leading overland. Overland trips in those days were the talk of OM. Everyone had heard about them but only a few actually participated. Those who did so were the brave ones, headed for uncharted territories in India and Bangladesh, braving hazardous journeys to reach their destinations. At a time when the centre of OM activities was in Europe travelling such distances was the call of the hardy, the elite and perhaps the lunatic.

Accounts of OM pioneers making the first overland trips were part of OM legend. We had all heard the stories of teams stranded on desert roads, of wheels immobilised by ice during the winter, of river-crossing without the aid of bridges, of finding ways through when roads disappeared and of attacks by bandits.

Why didn't we fly? Firstly, travelling overland was a lot cheaper, especially when we travelled in convoys. Secondly, this was a way to provide trucks and vans to meet the needs of the Indian travelling teams in the 1960s and 1970s. Lastly, the vans and trucks transported supplies of all sorts for our non-Indian workers, from western foodstuff and medicines, to 'Charlie' (the OM second-hand clothes supply).

Ken explained that since the *Logos* had not visited Asia for several years it would be the team's purpose to visit friends and partners to renew relationships. The main reason, however, was to spread the vision of the second ship, to raise prayers and prayer partners, and to recruit a new batch of workers when the vision became a reality. I had heard about the vision of the second ship several weeks before but had no idea how serious this talk had become in the leadership circle. I told Ken I would be delighted to join his team.

There were four on this team – all men. Ken was the team leader and first driver, John Diehl, an American, was the second driver. Frankie Low and I, both from Singapore, were the navigators. In addition, I was appointed team cook!

The OM vehicle base located in Zaventem just outside Brussels, Belgium, provided a vehicle for the trip. It was a six-wheel Ford Transit, larger than we expected. OM vehicles were old by normal standards and we were given the oldest of the old fleet. The chief mechanic who gave us the Ford told us that it was not necessary to return it. On arrival in Malaysia we could do whatever we wanted with it.

Before we set out on our trip the vehicle required some attention. We drove it down to the harbour in Antwerp where the *Logos* was berthed. The ship engineers welded a roof rack on to it and on this we sat several metal trunks for storage of equipment. Inside, just behind the driver and the front passenger seat, we propped up a table next to the two-person seat. A false floor was welded in the back of the Transit. The top would provide a sleeping area for three of us – Ken, John and I. Underneath would be storage space. Frankie, being the shortest of the team would sleep across the front seat. We carried a library of message tapes for our spiritual nourishment. Ken installed several points for headphones around the vehicle to help shut out the noise when we were listening to George Verwer, Billy Graham or A.W. Tozer on cassette while travelling.

The final task was to spray-paint the Transit – white at the top and sky-blue on the body, thus earning her name the *Blue Streak*. She turned out to be a mechanical nightmare, becoming a real test of our patience and trust in God. However when our team finally disbanded we had all developed an affectionate attachment to our 'miracle van' despite the problems she had given us.

We bade farewell to the ship in Rotterdam, Holland and drove the *Blue Streak* to Wassernaar, where the Second Ship Team had convened. There were about 70 people there, most of whom had served on the *Logos* and were convinced about the value of the ship ministry. We met together to pray, prepare and trust the Lord by faith, for a second ship.

The group included families, children, engineers, deck crew, ministry and programme personnel. One team had already left for Mexico to spread the vision about the second ship. It was the findings of the Mexico travelling team that later led to the *Doulos* spending a good number of years in Latin America resulting in a movement of missions among the Latin Churches.

We spent several days in prayer, fellowship and preparation before making our way back to Zaventem. Here we stocked up on food and fine-tuned the vehicle. The cook provided us with two drums of peanut butter, two drums of strawberry jam, two crates of Belgian apples, one drum of tomato soup powder and one drum of mashed potato powder (each drum was 5 kgs in size). We were also given a portable stove, kerosene, tow ropes, cooking utensils, jerrycans for extra fuel, jerrycans for water and a host of smaller items. I realised that as cook I would need a great deal of creativity if I were to vary my dishes! We planned to eat the relatively cheap local food once we had got beyond Austria, I thought this was a good plan!

It was approaching the end of October 1976, Ken was concerned that if we did not set out soon we might be stranded in the snow in the mountainous regions of eastern Turkey. After a short stay of four days in Zaventem we were on our way.

Chapter Five

It's a Long, Long Way Lord

*'It has always been my ambition to preach
the gospel where Christ was not known, so
that I would not be building on someone
else's foundation.'*
Romans 15:20

'Malaysia is a long, long way Lord!'

This was the prayer of Kees Rosies, then OM Benelux Leader, as we left the OM European Headquarters in Zaventem. I will never forget this poignant and candid prayer at the start of our journey of a lifetime. The fact that I lived to write about this is a testimony of God's protection and faithfulness. Kees' prayer was answered, we were protected from the dangers we found ourselves in.

We were not the only overland travellers on the roads at this time. En route we met fellow overlanders travelling by motorcycle, bus and in mini convoys of trucks and vans. There was a couple in a Range Rover (the way to go for the rich!), as well as drivers of container trucks ferrying goods between Europe and Asia. Then there was the intrepid individual we met riding a bicycle in the mountains of Afghanistan who had pedalled all the way from Finland!

While some overlanders travelled for the fun and adventure, many, during that hippie era, travelled for no particular reason. Perhaps they were in search of some fulfilment or purpose in life. Many were headed for India in the footsteps of The Beatles to find a Hindu guru with the answers to life. The Beatles themselves of course chose to travel by air.

Ken had chosen a route that all overlanders took at that time. Most travellers would end their journey in India but we would travel beyond, to Malaysia and Singapore. We obtained a detailed overland map and on studying it I was impressed by the information I found. Specific mileage was given between refuelling stations – this was extremely helpful in planning our journey, not once did we run out of diesel. Names of places on the map were given in English but we experienced few problems finding the cities, towns and villages in countries where English was not spoken. Except for a few occasions we hardly got seriously lost, the credit for this is probably due to the accuracy of the map rather than the skill of the navigators!

All in all the entire trip would cover 7,400 miles, or over 11,000 kilometres and would see us travelling through Germany, Austria, Yugoslavia, Greece, Turkey, Iran, Afghanistan, Pakistan, India, Bangladesh, back to India, by ferry to Malaysia, and Singapore. The dream of driving from Europe to Singapore was only broken by the absence of a road through Burma, now Myanmar. For this reason, we had to double back to India after Bangladesh, to catch a ferry in Madras.

The major cities on our way included Stuttgart, Innsbruck, Zagreb, Skopje, Thessalonica, Istanbul, Ankara, Tabriz, Tehran, Kabul, Lahore, Amritsar, New Delhi, Ahmedabad, Bombay, Belgaum, Bangalore, Cuttack, Calcutta, Dhaka, back to Calcutta, Madras, Penang and Klang in Malaysia.

We also called at lesser known towns and cities. Where possible we would enjoy fellowship with believers in churches and homes and had opportunities to join local OM teams in fellowship and outreach.

Was this the 10/40 Window that we were travelling in? Yes, for the most part, but this term, coined in the early 1990s, was not known then. The 10/40 Window is a term used to describe the section of the world 10 to 40 degrees latitude north of the equator, stretching from North Africa on the western edge to Japan on the eastern edge. It is often referred to as the last frontier for the Gospel in today's missions.

Our drive introduced me to places and peoples who could only be reached by Christians with pioneering spirit. The Church in countries like Turkey, Iran and Afghanistan, for instance, had only a handful of followers of Jesus Christ then. For those from countries where there is a sizeable Christian population it is very difficult to imagine the pressure, harassment and persecution that people in such places face as a minority. Through the years it has been my privilege and commitment to encourage prayers and people in the direction of this part of the world.

Let's get back to the overland journey. We'll begin with the most unpleasant experience and get it out of the way. As I have mentioned the *Blue Streak* turned out to be a disaster from day one. We had hundreds of stoppages along the way caused by air in the fuel pipes. When it happened we had to stop to bleed the pipes regardless of where we might be – on a country road or on the highway. Travelling with us was another vehicle with three men who were headed for Bangladesh; two were former deck officers. Max, an Australian, who was mechanically skilled, had the unpleasant job of blowing into the fuel tank every time bleeding was needed. One time, by the roadside in Iran, Max gave such a puff that the fuel came flooding out into his eyes. For a moment we thought we had a crisis on our hands in the middle of nowhere. Thankfully with a flush of water, Max regained his sight.

Another time, we had to remove the exhaust pipe as it had fallen out. It was the middle of the night and we were approaching Tehran, Iran. We got into the habit of parking the Transit on a slope so that we didn't have to push-start it – a push-start demanded all the strength we could muster!

The *Blue Streak* dampened the joy of travel. If we were to start over again, our team lamented, we would never use an old OM vehicle! Having said this we realised that our vehicle had taught us much about faith and trusting God. Mechanically speaking it was a miracle she kept going.

The fact that we made it to Malaysia eventually, and went on to criss-cross the Peninsula there, is a credit to the old lady's enduring quality. In Malaysia we actually felt proud of her. Malaysian friends viewed the *Blue Streak* with a fair amount of curiosity. This was because she was left-hand drive in a country of right-hand drive vehicles. She also displayed a Dutch numberplate and a foreign vehicle in the late 1970s was a rarity that easily attracted attention. Passengers who got the opportunity to ride in her marvelled at the in-drive, entertainment system. The headphones could be switched to an open system so that passengers could enjoy the latest in Christian music!

It was beginning to get cold as we left Europe. For more than a week as we drove through beautiful Austria with its golden autumn landscape, the drab countryside (the leaves had started to fall) of Yugoslavia, and the sometimes dusty roads of Greece, we did not stop for a bath – not even a wash. Public facilities were few and far between and we were trying to beat the winter in eastern Turkey. The good thing about the cold in contrast to the heat and humidity in the tropics, was that we did not feel sticky and uncomfortable although we were by no means fresh and clean. It was with eager anticipation that we arrived in Istanbul for our first Turkish bath.

I had never been in a Turkish bath before, so I was unprepared for the sight that greeted me as I walked into the hall. I was used to my army mates in their various stages of modesty when we were in the barracks, but going into a Turkish bath full of naked Turkish men was another matter. It was a culture shock!

In the middle of the steamy hall a number of men were laid on a marble platform. Having just come in from the cold outside, I was eager to feel the warmth the slab of marble offered. No sooner had my skin made contact with the marble slab though, than I jumped straight up, to the chagrin of the Turks around me. It wasn't warm; it was burning! I tried sitting down on it again, but a lot slower this time – it was more tolerable. The heat penetrated my body and did have a relieving effect. Nearby was a door with a small glass window. I did not know it was a sauna. I had never been in a sauna before. Pushing the door open, I walked in. The steam nearly knocked me out flat; it was suffocating. It took me several minutes to adjust but once I had it felt really good, especially after a week of accumulated dirt.

This ritual over I headed out to the row of taps. There I saw men in pairs taking turns to rub and scrub each other, soap and a wash were next, then back to rubbing and scrubbing until there was no dirt left. I was too embarrassed to ask any of my travelling companions to scrub me!

A Turkish bath is incomplete without a Turkish massage. There on tables, not unlike those found in a morgue, expert masseurs were at work. It looked rough handling to me. I was far too ticklish and self-conscious to dare a go.

On leaving the bath all four of us felt rejuvenated, refreshed and relaxed. We were ready for another indefinite period of travel-without-wash!

Whilst in Turkey we met some of our fellow-workers who were seeking ways to share the Gospel with the people in this country. I had first started praying for Turkey and its people a year before, on the MV *Logos*. I was inspired to do so on learning that there were less than 50 believers in Jesus Christ in a country of 50 million people. I have never ceased praying for Turkey since then. What a joy it was, when on my next visit

21 years later, I found the situation changed for the better. There are now more than a thousand believers in the country and whereas changing one's religion on one's identity card was unheard of as recently as a year or two ago, it is not against the law now.

There are other signs of the changed situation in Turkey. A Bible school has been set up and has a small group of Turkish students. Being the first they do not have any Turkish reference books or commentaries. In fact they are the ones who will produce the materials for the benefit of future students.

Last Christmas, the Turkish churches in partnership with the International Church held a Christmas (evangelistic) party at a hotel in the capital, Ankara. This was attended by more than a thousand people. Police permission was obtained and the police officer at the end suggested that the event be held in a larger venue next year! Progress made is the result of many years of plodding on in the work of God. It is all well worth the trouble and the heartache, even though the number of Christians remains negligible when compared to the ever-increasing population.

Travelling through the beautiful mountainous regions of eastern Turkey was a special treat. Years later this area would become the refuge for Kurdish people fleeing Iraq. The Kurdish people, who number approximately 20 million around the world, form the largest people group in the world without a country. Special though the mountainous region was, approaching Mount Ararat, the mountain that Noah's ark came to rest on (Gen. 8:4) was a highlight for us. Turkey is a long country from east to west and it took us three days and three nights to drive from Ankara to the border. Mount Ararat is situated right at the fringe of the eastern border of Turkey.

On rising the next morning we took time to admire the beauty of the snow-capped mountain, it was breathtaking. It took us an entire day to drive round the mountain's base. Before setting out we ate a hearty breakfast and had a time of prayer and praise. By now we had adapted to the Turkish bread. We would buy two loaves and these would last us for the day. We had also decided that we would only stop for a cooked meal in the evening. The bread was eaten at breakfast and lunch with a choice of peanut butter or jam, or both and surprisingly we actually enjoyed it.

Mount Ararat was awesome and the day was gloriously clear with crisp, cold air and a blue and cloudless sky. Throughout the day I imagined what it was like for Noah, his family and animals, streaming from the ark and down the mountain slopes. We strained our eyes to try and catch sight of the ancient ship, but of course several thousand years have effectively buried all traces of it.

The main road between Turkey and Iran was well used – over-used may be a better description – by container trucks carrying foodstuff between Europe and the Middle East. The Shah then ruled Iran and Iraq was not a problem as it is now, so there was much movement of goods. Driving on this narrow, over-crowded, fast road was a real test of nerves. Wreckages littered the roadside.

On approaching the Iranian border we discovered to our dismay that the queue of vehicles at the checkpoint was so long we couldn't see the front. Ken decided that as we were not a goods vehicle we could jump the entire queue. We drove straight up to Customs and Immigration.

The checkpoint hall was filled with acrid smoke from all kinds of cigarettes. The warmth of the immigration officers came as a refreshing surprise. They offered us a cup of tea and wanted to chat and so we chatted. With a cursory glance at our papers, the officers stamped everything – from passports and customs declaration to vehicle carnet. What we anticipated would be a painful process turned out to be a picnic. The Lord was good to grant favour from the officials, and this was just the start of His graciousness. We enjoyed hospitality in every subsequent checkpoint.

Iran under the Shah was more welcoming to foreigners than it proved to be under the rule of Ayatollah Khomeni. Shortly after Khomeni came to power OM ceased its overland trips as did many other overlanders. Iran was closed and proved to be inhospitable for travellers.

OM now uses air travel. What took a month by van now takes only ten hours! The record shortest time for an OM overland trip between Europe and India was 21 days, to achieve this the drivers took turns to drive non-stop.

Iran was as a typical Middle-Eastern country – very Islamic, rather conservative. I was not told of the existence of any church, although I was aware of work by several groups. It was a joy to find out in 1997, from an Iranian pastor, that there are several churches in the capital Tehran. Some churches are actively involved in outreach despite the pressure and persecution, several pastors have been martyred in recent years. A large part of this huge country remains unreached and poses one of the great challenges facing the outside Church.

Chapter Six

Up the Khyber

*'In the same way, the Spirit helps us in our
weakness. We do not know what we ought to pray
for, but the Spirit himself intercedes for us with
groans that words cannot express. And he who
searches our hearts knows the mind of the Spirit,
because the Spirit intercedes for the saints in
accordance with God's will.'*
Romans 8:26–27

I have a confession to make. I am still wearing
an 'L' plate on the road of prayer. Christians tend
to think prayer skills can be acquired but I think
this is too simplistic.

I have prayed all my Christian life. I have
prayed standing up and sitting down, I have
prayed with eyes closed and open. I have prayed
while jogging, swimming, cycling or working
out in the gym. If I am in a church I will blend
in with its praying culture. I have prayed for
good and bad people, for honest government and

crooked leaders. I have prayed for all kinds of situations – I pray for the crisis, just as I pray for the mundane.

I have read many books on prayer and met authors who have written about prayer. I have listened to countless cassettes on prayer and attended sessions on prayer. Sometimes I even preach about prayer myself!

I have seen instant answers to prayer as well as delayed answers. I have known prayers that are still unanswered. I have also heard all kinds of prayer uttered. Some funny, others intimate, some triumphalistic, others defeatist. Some full of faith, others filled with doubt. Many were earnest and countless were just plain repetitive.

Despite all this exposure I am still a novice in prayer. I know very little about prayer and praying. Thankfully I am in good company. I find it such a relief to know that Paul, obviously one of the giants of the faith, was able to say that he did not know what and how to pray (Rom. 8:26).

I have found that some books and articles on prayer are discouraging because they make prayer sound so mysterious and hard to grasp. Thankfully we have Jesus' teaching to help us on prayer. I find it refreshing and assuring to know that God is so accessible to us!

Afghanistan is one of those countries for which I have little idea how to pray. A fellow OM leader and his wife who have been involved with the

Afghans for the past 30 years recently admitted that it seems the more they pray for this country and its people the more the situation deteriorates. God seemed to have chosen not to work according to the way they pray. It was comforting to know that I was not the only person with this problem. Knowing how and what to pray is a common problem for people, as it was for Paul.

My knowledge of Afghanistan was limited when I joined OM. I remember someone sharing the depressing news about the first church built in Kabul, the capital, which had been bulldozed to the ground the following day. This was a country with 48,000 mosques and not a single church. Such information ignited a desire in me to be there.

Here I was, two years after hearing the news about the demolished church, about to enter the country. The Russians had not invaded yet. As we approached the Iran–Afghanistan border we noticed many warnings against smuggling drugs. Afghanistan was fertile ground for both the cultivation and trafficking of opium, the basic stuff from which heroin is derived.

Our strategy on approaching a checkpoint to cross a border was to shave and change into fresh clothes. We wanted to give the impression to customs and immigration officers that we were decent people (as we were!) and not suspicious-looking unkempt hikers who might be drug smugglers. As the border on the Iranian side had closed we slept in our vehicle that night.

It was very cold. Before I left the *Logos* someone had given me a thick sweater and a winter parka which I put on before crawling into my sleeping bag and piling several blankets on top – I was still freezing. It was a great relief when morning broke.

Stepping out of the vehicle we found a layer of frost on the dry ground. As luck would have it my scalp chose that morning to itch! So in sub-zero temperatures I trudged to the nearest public toilet. It only had one cubicle and a tap outside. I turned on the tap and icy water gushed out. I peeled off some layers of clothing and dipped my head under the tap. It was freezing cold. I quickly shampooed, rinsed and dried my hair in record time. It was quite a refreshing experience, although not as enjoyable as the Turkish bath.

Then it was time to cross the Afghan border. Ken had warned us that customs clearance could take as long as half a day and that checks would probably be thorough. Ken also, for the first time, disclosed to us that we had a trunkload of Afghan Scriptures to smuggle in. We prayed that they would not be confiscated.

The spartan checkpoint was little more than a hut, but the efficiency of its staff was great. The four of us, decent, clean-shaven and good-looking, approached the officer to have our passports stamped. A vehicle inspection followed. In

Malaysia and Singapore, sniffer dogs are used to sniff out drugs. Here a little Afghan boy was the drug-sniffer!

Once we had unloaded and displayed most of our luggage on the ground the boy got down to work. He went under the vehicle, climbed on top, crawled under the seats, and finally wriggled himself through the narrow confines under the false floor. Of course there were no drugs. We were sure about that as we had deliberately avoided picking up passengers along the way who might make use of our vehicle as a conduit for their contraband. But we were not so confident about the trunkload of Afghan Scriptures which was now supporting the foot of the customs officer. Thankfully the officer was satisfied with his search and waved us on without opening up the trunk. The Scriptures made it through, as miracles go it was a simple yet effective one!

Seized goods were displayed at the check-points; a pair of walking boots with the soles torn out to expose sachets of heroin, a gas stove cut open to expose a lump of opium. Another smuggler had hidden drugs in the metal frame of a backpack. Such ingenuity could not escape the experienced eye of the customs officers. Having crossed many borders in the course of my career with OM I remain amazed by the risks smugglers take. I think that in terms of knowing and seeing everything, customs officers come a close second to God!

Afghanistan's terrain was rugged and mountainous. Dry and inhospitable, the country gave one a sense of isolation and a feeling of despair. No wonder the Russians did not last long after their occupation of the land. Yet there was incredible beauty in much of the wilderness.

We stayed with a couple in Kabul. They showed me what pioneer work entailed. It was slow and hard work, often seemingly with little or no results. I had read stories of God's people serving in places like this who never experience reaping, despite the years of sowing God's Word. Perhaps the next generation/s will have the privilege of reaping what the pioneers have painstakingly sown. This couple, in my view, personified the pioneer spirit. They are still working in refugee camps seeking to share the liberating news of Jesus Christ with the Afghans.

We did not meet any other believers during our week there. I have not yet come into contact with a native Afghan who is a Christian, although I know there are a few believers outside of Afghanistan. This continues to motivate me to pray and trust the Lord for a late harvest.

Leaving Kabul we also left the winter cold behind for a warmer climate and came to the famous Khyber Pass. The views of the rugged, rocky and wild land were spectacular. About a dozen Afghan children jumped on our vehicle to hitch a ride down the mountain, the local bus was either unreliable or non-existent.

On arrival in Peshawar, Pakistan, we rested. A little boy who pointed a fountain pen at my face and asked me if I would like to buy a 'pen pistol' shocked me. It was a real gun and so I was relieved that he had not accidentally pulled the trigger.

Peshawar was fast becoming a bustling border town. Some years later, when the Russians invaded Afghanistan, hundreds of thousands of refugees crowded along this side of the Pakistan border. They have remained there since and Peshawar is the gateway city for them to hop to other parts of Pakistan and connect with the world. Ironically, because Pakistan was much more open than Afghanistan in carrying out the work of God, opportunities arose like never before, to reach out to the Afghans. Though we could not go to them, they came to us. God 'moves' in mysterious ways!

I am still following developments in Afghanistan. Instead of opening up, under the Taliban the country is getting increasingly militant and extreme. Women and children especially suffer greatly under the regime. I look forward to the day when workers can freely go in and out to share the good news of Jesus Christ. But until then we need to persevere in prayer. Pioneers and prayers are desperately needed for a country like Afghanistan.

Chapter Seven

Sea of Humanity

*'When he saw the crowds, he had compassion on
them, because they were harassed and helpless,
like sheep without a shepherd.'*
Matthew 9:36

No country in the world, except perhaps China,
has so much to offer civilisation as India.

With a population of 950 million and counting
it is expected to overtake the population of
China in the next 50 years; it is a country seeth-
ing with people. Its varied landscape, rich culture
and colourful people make it a photographer's
dream.

India is a country of sharp contrasts. Home of
the magnificent Taj Mahal and the appalling
Calcutta and Bombay slums, she shows the
extremes of wealth and poverty. She has her
spectacular mountains in the north, but also
the dry and barren deserts in the north-east.
There are the fair and light complexions of

those from Kashmir, and the brown skin of Tamilnadu.

Despite the poverty, there is so much to India that is positive, meaningful and endearing. I came away from India enriched.

The first time I set foot in India was when the MV *Logos* dry-docked there in 1975. Mentally and emotionally, I was ill prepared. I did not know how to deal with the never-ending stream of professional beggars of all ages. I could not handle the heat and the crowds, the dust and pollution. It took me a year to prepare my heart and spirit to return to India. This time not only did I learn to like the country, I learned to love it and do to this day.

After a brief stop in Amritsar, Punjab, we headed towards New Delhi. We then travelled on to Ajmer in Rajasthan. In Kota we stopped to spend a week or so working with an OM India team based there.

We found our way to the team accommodation without difficulty. It was a team with five men led by the short, dark and stout Marcus Chacko, who hailed from the state of Kerala. Our paths would cross several times in the next two decades. It is always a delight to meet up with Marcus, just as it was when we first met. He is one of those people blessed with an infectious smile.

He showed us to the place where the team lived. It was a garage situated in front of a primary school, whose students the team was trying to reach out to, with the blessing of the principal.

The garage was no more than 15 feet by 10 feet yet the team slept, cooked and held their meetings here. I was stunned by its simplicity. Perhaps I should not have been so stunned as my home was the *Blue Streak*. Even then, our mobile home was a luxury compared to their all-purpose garage. The school classroom served as our bedroom for the week we were in Kota.

Early next morning, I awoke to an unusual scene. A steady stream of people holding small metal pots of water were walking past the school. The team told me that they were on their way to the communal toilet. The communal toilet, I discovered later, was a bush a little further down the path. The water pots were for washing, no toilet paper needed. I decided to use the school lavatory!

Sunil, one of the team members, and I hit it off from the start. At twenty-one he was two years younger than me. One morning, we cycled into town to distribute some literature. In no time, our bags were empty. That was the fun of tracting in India. There were always more people than literature available. Everyone took tracts and kept them – absolutely no wastage. We were on our way back to the garage when we came across a 'hotel' (the name for any 'chai' or teashop in

India) overlooking a lake. I suggested some refreshment and Sunil readily agreed.

As we were talking and relaxing I saw some squirrels playing near the metal railing at the edge of the lake. I ran towards them to see what their reaction would be. Of course they took flight when they saw me. I failed to notice the live wire hanging loose from the public lamp-post that was resting on the railing. As I touched the railing a surge of electric current exploded through my body.

I tried to extricate myself from the railing but could not get my hands free. I cried out to the Lord for help. In a flash I saw my life replayed right before my eyes. At that point I felt at peace with God. Having failed in tearing free, I told God that I was prepared to die. I asked for His forgiveness and cleansing. Then I asked Him to take me to Him; I was ready to meet God. All these thoughts raced through my mind in microseconds. As soon as I uttered that prayer I was flung back several feet. I lay there recovering from the shock. My body began to shake uncontrollably.

Sunil ran up to ask what was wrong, I told him to stand back and not to touch me. Sunil told me afterwards that I was grimacing but he thought I was only joking.

The fact that I am writing about the electrifying experience shows that I survived but this event did have a lasting effect upon me. I cried tears of relief, of joy and peace. I would always look back at this incident and remember that it was in Kota, India, that God gave me another chance to live for Him.

Our next stop was Ahmedabad, capital of Gujarat. What impressed me most as I travelled through the north-eastern part of India was the dire spiritual need. Churches were few and far between. Even today, the state of Uttar Pradesh, where 140 million live, has only 170 small churches. That works out to an average of one church for one million people. This fact and seeing the need myself continue to motivate me in prayer and in mobilising people and resources to that part of India.

Bombay is a mega-city teeming with humanity. There are lawyers, doctors, teachers, students, civil servants and traders, child labourers, prostitutes, pimps, syndicate operators, money-lenders, money-changers, shopkeepers and food deliverers.

Buses, trucks, cars, carts, bicycles, taxis, auto-rickshaws, bullock carts, cows, cattle, goats, you name it, all vie for a piece of the public roads. The famous Victoria Station for long-distance trains is packed with people 24 hours a day. The city mass transit system for office workers was quite an experience. During the peak hours in the morning and evening crowds packed into it tighter than sardines in a can, with perhaps half of the passengers hanging outside and topside!

The OM base was in NanaChouk, an old three-storey building in a quiet compound next to a college. It provided welcome refuge from the crowd and traffic just beyond the compound wall. Ray and Christa Eicher, veteran OMers, ran the operations in India out of this humble building. As soon as we were settled Ray informed us that a Pastors' Conference had been organised for the following Saturday. What came next left me trembling in terror. Ken asked me to give a message on world missions at the conference. After some consideration, I consented and spent the next two days worrying about what I should say. I had never preached a full-length message in English, and certainly not to a group of pastors.

Saturday came and so did the dreaded moment. I cannot remember what I said but I do remember my knees shaking uncontrollably.

After my message Ray made a comment that has stayed with me. His kind words meant so much to a first-time fumbling speaker who was convinced he had given the worst message ever. He said that what I shared had ministered to him and he wanted to express his appreciation for it. I was about to go somewhere and pray that the earth would swallow me up but Ray's encouragement helped turn me around. It was like a lifeline. To this day I continue to be sympathetic to people who preach God's Word. I believe we can learn something even from the most boring speaker – because that was what I was.

Goa, a former Portuguese enclave, was our next stop. We met many hippies on its beaches. The barter of drugs was common and one hippie informed me that there was a 'market' day and asked if I was interested in going. I was not. After several days of ministry we moved on to Belgaum.

Here we stayed with Dr Rajput, former medical officer of the MV *Logos*. His two lovely daughters and an OM women's team of foreigners made our stay very pleasant. Of course we observed the OM India social policy, which was a lot stricter than the ship's, but under the watchful eye of Dr and Mrs Rajput, we enjoyed the good company and fellowship.

We headed down to Bangalore en route towards Andhra Pradesh. We later stopped in Cuttack before arriving at Calcutta.

Calcutta holds a great fascination for me. It is like a place frozen in time and history. Calcutta is probably the only place in the world where the hand-pulled Chinese rickshaw is still used. The famous Howrah Bridge spanning the Hooghly River completely blew my mind. Every mode of transport imaginable used this bridge, which was straining under the weight, every minute of the hour, every hour of the day. I was told an estimated two million crossed the bridge each day. This was approximately the population of Singapore in 1977! Imagine the population of Singapore crossing the bridge every day! I heard of OM teams bracing themselves at one end of the bridge distributing tracts. Each person carried several bags shouting the different languages available – Hindi, Urdu, Oriya, Marathi and so on. Thousands of tracts disappeared very quickly.

Several years later I was on board the MV *Logos* when it arrived in Calcutta from Chittagong on Christmas Eve. I quickly organised an outing for the Chinese on board to a Chinese restaurant as a Christmas present to all of them. We walked three kilometres to and from the restaurant through the Calcutta Christmas crowd. It was a quick baptism to India for those who were there for the first time. The food was cheap and good.

One morning I was looking over the side of the ship as she was berthed at the Man-O-War jetty along the Hooghly River. A lot of rubbish was caught between the ship and the jetty and the stench coming from the rubbish was unbearable. Out of curiosity I went to check out why this was so. To my horror I found human carcasses and parts of human bodies stuck under the jetty. The Hooghly is a tributary of the holy Ganges River. Many people who had died up river had their bodies cremated. What I saw were the unburned remains that had floated downstream. A few moments later a Swiss lady who had joined me looked down and saw a human head with an upturned face staring at her. She gave a scream! A short distance away, a boatman laughed and continued brushing his teeth with a twig and gargling happily with a cup filled with river water!

In Calcutta, Matthew 9:36, which speaks of Jesus' compassion for the crowds, was of special importance to me. When faced with such a vast sea of humanity there are only two options to choose from – to get out of the city in the quickest possible time or, like Jesus, to be moved with compassion. I had learned to accept what was there. I was even fascinated by the sheer experience of being there. Beyond all this the Lord was teaching me that I should love people as they are. This is a lesson that I have often had to relearn through the years.

One afternoon, as I was walking along a busy road in the city, I came across an empty plot of land between two old houses. On it was a huge heap of refuse, piled as high as the first storey of the adjacent buildings. On top of the heap were several vultures and a number of crows, scavenging for the little that was edible. What I saw at the foot of the heap broke my heart. There were children and women picking through the refuse searching for something to eat or to sell. Little boys and girls were picking up scraps of rejected vegetables and rice grain to take home. Home often was just a few pieces of cardboard assembled together.

That night I could neither eat nor sleep. I got on my knees to pray and I believe the Lord broke and softened my hardened heart. I believe He used what I saw that day to bring the dimension of compassion into my life. I promised the Lord that, for the rest of my life, I would always be grateful to Him for what He would provide for me. I promised Him that not only would I be more generous but that I would accept and not grumble over what was to be my lot. Through the years there have been times when I have slid back to grumbling and dissatisfaction, but thankfully such times have been few and far between.

The overland trip taught me a lot which has stood me in good stead as I have sought to live a life as a true follower of Jesus Christ. Though the trip introduced me to some of the most gruelling places in the world as far as the Gospel is concerned, it was by no means the end. I have since had the privilege and honour of working in partnership with those who live and work in some of these places, people who in my estimation, rank close to those we read of in Hebrews 11 – the heroes and heroines of faith.

Chapter Eight

Down by the River

*'Foxes have holes and birds of the air have
nests, but the Son of Man has no place to lay
his head.'*
Matthew 8:20

Life is complicated. Living in an affluent society
adds to the problem. The rat race, materialism,
keeping up with the Tans (the Chinese version
of the Joneses) and the five Cs (car, credit card,
cash, condominium and club membership) can
become all-important. In such an environment it
is not easy to opt for contentment and simplicity
in our lifestyle.

There is beauty in simplicity. Architects live
by it, artists breathe in it and poets attest to it.
My wife's uncle is a famous sculptor in Singapore
who introduced me to the art of 'omission in
sculpture' – using the minimum to express the
most. His pieces are outstandingly and decep-
tively simple.

I was not rich and am still not rich, going by the average standard in my society. Wealth is of course relative, and often it is deceptive too. It is deceptive because the lack or abundance of it does not say much about the condition of the heart.

My pilgrimage in the virtue of contentment began when my life was touched by others who were very poor, at least by my standards, but whose lives greatly enriched my own. Chuni, Hebol, Anup and Serjent were just some of the Bangladeshi brothers who exemplified this virtue in truth and in reality.

The overland team was about to disband, having achieved what we had set out to do. It had been nine months since we set off from Holland and we had recruited as many as 70 new workers, many of whom would end up as pioneers several months later on the second ship, the MV *Doulos*.

Each team member had their own plans. John was going to Germany to marry, Frankie was off to Singapore to look after the *Logos* office there, and Ken was returning to Europe before setting out to India to prepare for the visit of the *Logos*. The *Blue Streak*, our Ford Transit, was given to a small group of people in Klang, Malaysia.

I however had no plans, I was simply willing and available to let God use me in any way He wanted. I knew He would lead me and I was ready and eager to do His bidding. As a single young man my faith was quite simple and straightforward.

Ken asked me if I would like to be part of his team in November or December of that year when he planned to be in Gujurat, India, preparing for the return of the *Logos*. Without much hesitation I accepted this invitation as a direction from the Lord. Asians do not normally make quick decisions. First of all our parents and church leaders have to be consulted. However both my parents died some years back, and although my eldest sister who acted as my guardian objected, thinking that I was throwing away a 'proper' career, she left the decision to me (later, she became one of my strongest supporters). Missions was fairly new and volunteers to missions were few in the Singapore church in the 1970s. When a young man like me offered to continue in missions my former home church was more than willing to give its approval.

As it was now May I had six months to fill. 'Why don't you go to Bangladesh?' suggested Ken, 'You enjoyed it when we were there, and Mike Lyth could do with an extra pair of hands.' Bangladesh was an entirely new proposition, but it did not take me long to decide to proceed. I began making travel arrangements.

Now that I was on my own every dollar counted. I would travel by train from Singapore to Bangkok and then fly budget airline to Dhaka.

You could not travel any cheaper than that! After paying for the tickets I had only 70 US dollars left. With only a backpack and a sleeping bag I boarded the train in Singapore. It pulled into Bangkok a day and a half later. I spent a day in the city before catching the flight to Dhaka. Mike Lyth, the leader of OM's ministry there, met me at the airport. He drove me straight to our base along Green Road.

The Bangladesh ministry consisted of several teams made up of local brothers. Bangladeshi society is a man's world, so we only had male teams. Men reached out to men with the Gospel, never to women. Only women could reach out to women. Any other way would be inappropriate in that culture and severely frowned upon. Also, in that culture it was difficult, if not impossible, to recruit young women and have them travel around the country in itinerant ministry. Several men's teams were already involved in outreach and working among the Bangladeshi churches. Was I to join one of these teams?

The answer was no as Mike was going to try out a new approach. He wanted to launch a boat team! The rationale behind it was simple, there were more rivers than roads in the country and during the monsoon season each year it would rain non-stop for two or three months from July to September. A boat was then the best mode of transport. If OM had one it could continue its Gospel tract distribution and team ministry.

Mike had already bought a boat; it was sitting in the porch of the new base. Made of fibreglass, it was 17 feet long and slightly damaged with a few gaping holes on the hull. It was also bare and empty.

Mike dropped the bombshell that he wanted the boat ready before the monsoon came. I nearly stumbled over my backpack that was still sitting in the driveway. To my relief he quickly added that there would be a small team working with me. He then introduced me to Chuni Mondol and Hebol, both Bangladeshi men who would be in charge of the team.

The list of work included giving the boat a new coat of paint, patching the holes on the hull, installing floorboards to create storage space for Scriptures, erecting a coconut/bamboo roof to provide shelter and protection and mounting an outboard motor.

My task was to patch up the holes with fibreglass. I had absolutely no idea what was needed for the job but did not admit my ignorance. I did not want Mike to know that Ken had recommended a fellow from a big ship with little knowledge of how to fix a small boat! My pride dictated that, by hook or by crook, I had to resolve my mini-crisis myself – and quickly. A shop selling fibreglass repair kits provided the solution. I studied and scrutinised the kit instructions until I was absolutely certain what needed to be done. Tentatively I began mixing the powder and the fibre, while pouring in some glue. After patching up the first hole I was quite pleased with my handiwork. Before the day was done all holes had been patched. I am proud to say that the boat stayed afloat all the time she was in service.

After several weeks, as if perfectly timed, the monsoon began just as the boat was ready. Rivers and streams rose to a height of 12 feet. What paddy-fields with small mounds of settlements one saw during the dry season would be swallowed up, transformed into seas of water and islands of huts. Such was the deluge in this country that every year the rain and floods would cause the loss of many lives and properties. Yet the people are resilient, they keep living on, year after year, monsoon after monsoon.

Nothing stays dry for long during the monsoon season. Unpleasant things thrive in dampness, fungus being one of them. To prevent fungus from staining our clothes we placed lightbulbs in our cupboards in the knowledge that the heat would keep them dry.

It was time to launch the boat. As we arrived at the river a crowd began to gather despite the heavy rain. We loaded hundreds of copies of the newly printed *Common Bengali New Testament* – a translation that proved to be very popular. Chuni, Hebol, Horen, David and I, plus a live chicken, formed the boat team. The chicken came along as our thoughtful Bengali cook, with the English-sounding name of Steward (probably given to him as he was the steward of the household), wanted to make sure we had fresh meat to eat. We stocked up on rice and some dried foodstuff. Mike prayed and committed us into God's hand, Chuni revved up the outboard motor and we were on our way.

Our destination was Chunkuri, Chuni's home village, in District Khulna, which was about 150 km by river. We were excited about the trip. We felt that we were launching into a new era of modern transportation, at least by Bangladeshi standards. We were delighted that in a small way, we were trusting the Lord for a unique tool we could use to speed up the distribution of His Word. It was not unlike the idea of the MV *Logos* as an ocean-going ship bringing the Gospel to countries around the world.

I am impressed by the way God works through simple ideas. The ship ministry came about when a group of people praying over a world map noticed the vast expanse of sea and ocean covering the world and came up with the idea of a mission ship. Six years later they bought a ship and staffed it with a Christian crew. In our case in Bangladesh, with so many rivers, why not a Gospel boat? So there we were.

After several hours of travel we came to the edge of the Jamuna River, a tributary of the River

Ganges. As darkness fell we pulled alongside some river huts to spend the night. Mosquitoes descended upon us. We spread open our mosquito net but it could not accommodate five burly men comfortably and I ended up sleeping at an awkward angle with my head sticking out at the bow. None of us had a good sleep. The following morning I awoke to the noise of crows, which were swooping down towards me. It occurred to me that these scavengers thought I was dead meat ready for picking. Or perhaps they were after the food available from the rubbish dump next to where our boat was berthed!

For our travels we had managed to obtain a map of Bangladesh but to play safe we usually asked fellow boatmen for confirmation of routes. The most challenging sector lay ahead of us. Jamuna River is fast flowing, several miles wide and has strong currents. From where we stood we could not make out where the opposite bank was. Chuni and Hebol took the brave decision to go by instinct. It had to be right ahead. As long as we were travelling perpendicular to the currents we should be all right. There was great relief when we sighted the river mouth at the precise spot we had hoped for!

The following week saw us chugging through the maze of rivers. The river transport system was primitive. Some junks, laden with bricks, with gunwales almost at water level, were being pulled by men on the riverbank. Progress was obviously slow and laborious. It did not help that the wind had died down completely. Life went on simply, sedately. It was like travelling back in time. I could picture William Carey waiting at the riverbank for a boat to come along and pick him up.

I have learned to admire the resolve of the Bangladeshis through the years. They are hard-working, they are rebuilders and survivors. To be sure, there is plenty of hardship and suffering, but God is using people like Chuni, Hebol and Serjent to bring hope to their people. Horen, the youngest on the boat team, died when he was run over by a train several years later. No one knew if he fell by accident or if he was pushed. Building and rebuilding of lives take place all the time. In a place like Bangladesh survival is ingrained in the spirit. Whatever the inevi-tabilities of life, life itself continues.

We stopped at villages for pratas and vegetables to eat. David did not slaughter the chicken the way I expected it to be done. To ensure a clean job he skinned the bird with all its feathers still intact. We had a kerosene stove for cooking and chicken curry was served that evening. By now we had learned to sleep on top of the thatched roof. Chuni, Hebol and I took turns to steer the outboard motor. Life was care-free for us. We were all dressed in lungis – a type of loincloth worn by the typical Indian.

For our daily bath we dived into the river. It was amazing how refreshing a river bath could be even though the water was muddy brown. I was told that as long as it was not stagnant, but moving, the water should be safe enough to swim or bathe in, but not to drink. We obtained cleaner water onshore from water wells. For toilet visits we used clumps of bushes on the bank or waited for a bunch of floating weeds. No toilet paper was necessary.

We stopped several times at villages to sell at cost some of the New Testament books. After two weeks of travel we finally arrived at Chunkuri. Chuni's family was extremely hospitable. Village Chunkuri, as it was called, sat on an island, connected to the mainland only by a coconut tree-trunk. The extended family lived on this island. Huts had mud walls and thatched roofs. It was a Christian village and hygiene was good.

Tired from all the travelling, the dry and steady beds were irresistible. We simply collapsed into them. Early the following morning Chuni's mother woke me asking if I would like some tea. Breakfast in bed, now how about that! I had hot tea and a typical breakfast of pop-rice with green sugar bits. Turtle curry was served for lunch and it was delicious.

We explored the island later that day. It was peaceful, yet so vulnerable to the ravages of nature. We saw a flock of a dozen or so vultures.

When these scavengers circled in flight, you knew there was something dead or dying. They were huge ugly birds. I had seen how vultures in India went into a frenzy while feeding on a carcass – it did not take me long to develop a dislike for them.

After the boat mission I left the team to return to Dhaka. When I returned to base after being away for three weeks, a relieved Mike met me. He had not heard from us and had wondered whether we were dead or alive. With God's grace, we had survived.

The boat ministry continued and soon another boat was added to the 'fleet'. But due to the increasing accessibility of the country through the years ministries like ours had to adjust. In time the boat ministry became irrelevant, ending a most fruitful and ingenious way of getting the Word of God into the hands of the average Bangladeshi.

Chapter Nine

Bread, Cheese and Cornflakes

'Then Peter began to speak: "I now realise how
true it is that God does not show favouritism
but accepts men from every nation who fear
him and do what is right."'
Acts 10:34

Cross-cultural missions involve movement of
workers from one culture to another. The main
focus has been on the unreached peoples of the
world, meaning those people living in areas
where there is very little or no information on
the Gospel of Jesus Christ. UM has moved along
with this trend. From just providing a basic
training programme, it has now established
many avenues to help volunteers who want to
reach the unreached. Interestingly enough the
move towards cross-cultural missions happened
almost by default.

As the MV *Logos* sailed around South-East and
East Asia, it was greatly used by God as a catalyst

in motivating and mobilising the many churches
in Asia to missions. At a time when missions was
understood as what we received from the West
the ship was challenging many Asians to be more
outward-looking. Asian churches, we felt, should
not continue to think in terms of receiving, but
in terms of giving, both their people and
resources. This message was given everywhere
the ship went. As a result we saw more people
responding and wanting to join the ship ministry.
However, the maximum capacity of the ship for
both crew and staff was 140. Where else could
we channel the increasing number of people who
had volunteered, apart from the MV *Logos*?

The challenge was to open up the whole of OM
to them. As well as solving our placement
problem this would facilitate areas of work in
the former Indian subcontinent, Europe and the
Middle East. More importantly, it would widen
the vision of the Asian church. The responsibility
for this fell on the shoulders of two men – Allan
Adams, then instrumental in the recruitment of
Asians, and George Miley, then Director of MV
Logos.

Many questions were considered and re-
considered, even after the first decision was made
to send Asians beyond the ship. Would it be too
much to send new recruits to other countries at a
time few had thought of using short-term
workers? Would they survive in another country
and culture? Would they be a hindrance to those

engaged in long-term work? How were we going to prepare them for land teams and land work in other countries? How would OM, dominated as it was then by Europeans, respond to such an idea – would they welcome it? Would the Asian church consider elsewhere (other than Asia) a mission field? The questions were many, and so were the doubts. In the end, we felt that unless we tried, we would never find the answers.

So in 1976 the first batch of about forty recruits arrived in Europe for the European Summer Campaign. This annual affair, held every summer, was OM's way of mobilising Europeans, especially students, during the summer holidays, to reach out to Europe with the Gospel. Every year several thousand were mobilised for this purpose. It gave new recruits an opportunity for some initial training in evangelism and cross-cultural team living.

All who wanted to join OM at that time needed to have attended this campaign. It became the screening process to determine the suitability of new recruits for longer missions. A very few who had tremendous difficulty in Europe were sent home. Such decisions were very hard to make, but thankfully rare

Asians from Singapore, Malaysia, Australia, New Zealand and the Philippines underwent the summer experience. After that, everyone would attend the autumn conference. It was here that every leader from OM and every new recruit would meet to talk, pray and make the decision about where to go to serve for the year.

It was a new day, a fresh beginning, for the Asians. Instead of coming to Europe for a holiday or to study, they came to share the Gospel. It was not easy to convince families, church and friends back home about this. Even today the same grumbles are heard. Why Europe? It was not only expensive; it was a waste of time. After all, Europe did not need the Gospel – it gave us the Gospel! Europe was a Christian continent; we needed them more than they needed us.

The stark information we received about the church and situation in Europe however was depressing. In countries like Spain, Portugal, France and Italy, where the majority called themselves Roman Catholic, there were very few evangelical churches. Southern Europe – particularly France, Spain and Italy – was, and still is, in dire need of a spiritual uplift. One can travel to this part of Europe today, as most OMers do, and still find very few Bible-believing churches. Europe is a post-Christian continent, desperately in need of the Gospel. It needs re-evangelising.

This was an eye-opener for the Asians. You may think Christians are in the minority in Asia, but let me assure you that compared with Europe the Asian church is growing far faster.

There was also the challenge of Eastern Europe. Summer teams throughout the years were involved in smuggling Christian literature into these countries. Long-term workers too were involved in such smuggling. Due to the risks involved team members were quite prepared to spend some time in prison and some actually did. It was a remarkable day when the Berlin Wall fell in 1989. Today our teams continue in a more open atmosphere, although not entirely without restrictions, in some of these former communist regimes.

My job for seven summers from 1978 onwards was to lead groups of new recruits to Europe. Taking care of a party of 60 or 70 people at one time was fun but hard work. Departures were chaotic; if say 30 Singaporeans joined at that time, you could be assured that 30 churches and families would turn up to say goodbye at the airport. We created pandemonium at the old Paya Lebar Airport in Singapore each July when recruits left.

We took the cheapest possible airline one-way to Belgium. In the 1970s there were no long-haul flights, airlines stopped as many as three times along the route. Whenever we needed to change flight in Moscow, Prague or Bucharest, we were subjected to thorough searches as soldiers with sub-machine guns stood watch over us. Arrival in Zaventem, Belgium, was always a huge relief.

The Summer Campaign always began with a conference of a week's duration. The speakers at this conference were OM founder, George Verwer, co-founder, Dale Rhoton and then

European Co-ordinator, Jonathan McCrostie, who almost single-handedly co-ordinated all the summer events. Many of us were heartbroken when we heard that Jonathan had been badly injured in an accident in Spain. He is now wheelchair bound, but this has not stopped his contribution to the work in Europe.

The speakers motivated recruits to commitment and evangelism; the recruits also received training and orientation. If there were 20 countries or ministries vying for recruits, recruits would have 20 leaders challenging them to come and work in their respective countries or ministries. There was no shortage of variety. By the middle of the week it was all too common to have Asians utterly confused by the rich options available. Some even started panicking because the end of the week was fast approaching, and they did not want to end up with nowhere to go. It was my job to make sure they found the right placement.

There were teams remaining in Belgium working among students in university cities like Leuven and among immigrants in Brussels. For several years there was a summer blitz focusing on France. Of the 38,000 towns and villages, 36,000 do not have an evangelical witness. In Italy evangelical churches are small and few and far between. Teams lived and worked in areas where there were no churches. Accommodation one year was in tents pitched in a vineyard. We had

Italian pizza, pasta and fresh wine served at every meal!

There were also teams working among the Turks in Switzerland and Germany. The more daring ones travelled all the way to Turkey, where their summer was spent on the run, literally. They would travel from one place to another dropping literature and correspondence course material in mailboxes. One Malaysian, Ta Keng, was refused entry to Turkey. He left the team at the border and with little money left, hitchhiked all the way through Greece, Yugoslavia, Austria, Germany and back to Belgium. To this day, Ta Keng still remembers how, by faith, he trusted the Lord every step of the way.

My lifestyle was simple then; I was first introduced to bread, cheese and cornflakes at OM conferences. The cash I carried was limited and a visit to a restaurant was out of the question. I concluded that OM conference food was equivalent to the standard European diet. It was only much later when I tasted proper European food in the homes of friends and colleagues that I realised my mistake. I even got to enjoy the so-called 'bland' English food.

Cross-cultural assimilation begins with the stomach and we Asians had a hard time. We had bread and cornflakes for breakfast. Lunch was the main meal of the day; it included something hot, with bread. Dinner was bread and some soup. All the Asians were suffering.

By dinnertime we would be famished. In order to combat hunger and make it through to the next breakfast we would stuff ourselves with bread. A summer of bread certainly took its toll on our waistlines!

The element of trusting the Lord in OM was very strong. It still is. It was quite common to send teams out with a van or truck, with just enough money for diesel one-way, with a load of literature. The idea was to sell the literature and buy food with the proceeds. One team in France had such a difficult time in selling books that they went without food for some time. They were desperately hungry. As they were travelling along, wondering where the next meal would come from in a place where there was very little chance of Christian hospitality, the driver drove the van into a ditch. As they stepped out to check the damage they found, to their amazement, a hamper of fresh sandwiches, in the ditch. It must have fallen off someone else's vehicle. They accepted the food as God's provision. As soon as they had finished enjoying their first meal for several days a tractor came along and pulled them out of the ditch. You can imagine how precious such lessons of God's faithfulness are to those just starting out in living by faith.

In those early years of the 'invasion' of the Asian OMers little thought was given to orientation before the cross-cultural experience. With feedback from the pioneer batches we were able to give more information to new recruits. Even with such preparation culture shock was still a problem.

What were some of the cultural adjustments necessary? The European traffic system was certainly the first thing to adjust to. For people who were used to driving on the left side of the road, it was a major adjustment to a road system where drivers drive on the right side. It can be dangerous crossing the road and looking in the wrong direction. Every Asian who dared to drive an OM vehicle admitted that they had driven on the wrong side at least once! Mercifully these incidents happened on roads with light traffic.

Long summer days were another disorientation. Used to a consistent 12-hour period of daylight, this took the Asians some getting used to. They were left wondering why they were feeling so sleepy when it was still bright at 9.30 pm and why they were waking up in bright sunlight at 5.00 am.

Siesta in countries like Spain and Italy was also a new adjustment. All activities ceased for four hours from noon, then everything resumed. I was once on a team in Seville, Spain, which took lunch at 4.00 pm and dinner at midnight!

Coming from the teetotal Christianity of the East, we struggled with the relaxed European attitude towards alcohol. It was common to find wine at dinner tables in Christian homes and even more common to be served a glass of beer.

This is hardly an issue in the Bible, but it is amazing the sentiments and emotions it can arouse in people.

One of the funniest incidents of cultural assumption I experienced was in Liverpool, the first place I visited in the UK while serving on the MV *Logos*. We arrived in the summer of 1976 and I joined a team to minister in a church, partly motivated by the promise of an English meal. It was summer time and after the meeting, around 4.00 pm, we adjourned to the garden of the parish home of the vicar. We were served tea, the beverage that the British are famous for. There was also finger food – sandwiches, biscuits, scones and pastries. As this was only a snack, my team only nibbled at the delicacies leaving room in our stomachs for dinner. By 5.00 pm there was still no sign of any 'proper' food, 5.30 pm passed, and still nothing. That was when we were tactfully asked if we had to be back on the ship by the Merseyside hostess, who by then must have been wondering why we were lingering so long, while we were wondering when the food was going to arrive!

Most Asians come from consistently warm countries. As such we need only summer clothes. Preparation for the European autumn and winter was not easy; we could only guess what would be sufficient to keep us warm. I would arrange for those who did not have sufficient warm clothing with them to go to the Zaventem OM

European headquarters' second-hand clothes store 'Charlie'.

'Charlie' sometimes yielded fashion surprises for us. The fortunate and the quick would get hold of fairly new stuff of the right size and colour. Asian clothes are generally several sizes smaller than European ones. Some of the ladies ventured into the children's section to find clothes that fitted. Sometimes we did not know how to differentiate what were male and female clothes. Imagine an Asian guy wearing a woman's sweater with buttons fastening the 'wrong' side!

Another major change was hygiene. Asian and European practices differ. While Asians will shower before going to sleep at night after a hot and sticky day, Europeans prefer to bathe in the morning so that they will start the day fresh and clean. One good thing is that when you put several Asians and Europeans together on an OM team, you do not have the problem of everyone wanting the bathroom at the same time! As the European weather is generally dry and cool, even in summer, one does not feel as sticky as in the humid tropics. It did not take me long to discover that it was quite normal for Europeans to bathe once every few days, whereas Asians would do it daily. I was a guest in a German home once, and in order to avoid any inconvenience to my hostess, I asked her when would be a good time to use the shower. Expecting her answer to be a particular time of the day, I was taken aback when she said 'Saturday'.

Experiences in a European culture helped us to determine whether or not we had the ability to survive in another, perhaps more difficult, culture and in the missions context, to be effective in the work of the Gospel. It took us out of our comfort zone and this had a certain effect on our lives and attitudes. At worst, people got tired and gave up adapting; at best, we were better prepared for the life of missions in another vastly differing culture. The experience certainly helped us to appreciate others who had come to our own country and the cross-cultural process they had to go through in order to mingle with us.

Asians also received a crash course in language learning. We had to memorise phrases explaining who we were, we had to stress that we were neither Jehovah's Witnesses nor Children of God (both cult groups were very active in some countries), but sent from the local church, if there was one, or believers of Jesus Christ. Any more than this we had to refer to local believers or other team members. As there were many Europeans on the teams, the chances of one of them speaking the local language were very high.

We did a lot of open-air preaching on street corners and in parks. The group would sing in the hope of attracting a crowd, but often the sight of our international group was enough to arouse curiosity. Door-to-door outreach was most challenging in countries where privacy is jealously guarded. Apartment blocks would have a security guard or a door that only opened to residents. It took ingenuity to get into such premises. Even then teams were not welcome. A team in France had to contend with dogs. Their favourite verse was 'Watch out for those dogs . . . those mutilators of the flesh' (Phil. 3:2)!

By the 1980s teams were using mime and drama, music concerts and other creative means which have proved to be effective even to this day.

As English was the language they were comfortable with, many of the Asians chose to work in the UK, among the immigrants from the Middle East, South Asia and India. Work involved door-to-door visiting, showing videos, tea or curry parties, international evenings and so on. For those considering working in the countries these immigrants came from, it was a taste of those cultures and an opportunity to gauge one's attitude and readiness to make the necessary adjustments. Often this opportunity actually confirmed their unreadiness, in which case recruits would go somewhere else more suitable.

The feedback we received from the Asians was almost always positive. Many appreciated the opportunity to live by faith, to trust the Lord, to sow the seed of the Gospel, and even to lead someone to the Lord. Working in an international team for the first time also taught them many things about love, acceptance, unity and prayer. European OM leaders were appreciative of the extra dimension which the Asians brought to OM's ministry. Such a mutually beneficial arrangement and the fact that Europe remains one of the greatest challenges in missions today, mean that OM continues to challenge and channel people there.

Since 1976 thousands from Asia and the Pacific regions have participated and continue to participate in the Summer Campaign, now renamed 'Love Europe'. After each Summer Campaign, recruits regroup in Belgium for a time of prayer, of waiting upon the Lord, to decide on their course of action for the next two years. Asians have chosen to work in places like Europe, the Middle East, India, Pakistan, Central Asia, Bangladesh, North Africa, and on board the *Logos* and the *Doulos*.

It is my privilege and delight to find many from the East Asia Pacific region in key leadership positions around OM. Some of them are Field Leaders in their own right. A Korean brother is responsible for one of the fields in North Africa, while another Korean leads the work in a country in West Asia. An Australian, a Malaysian and a New Zealander each lead a ministry in the Middle East. Another Australian directs our work in Russia, while his Brisbane counterpart has taken over as Director of the

Doulos, with several other Asians in major leadership. In addition, all 12 offices in East Asia Pacific are led by nationals – people who have participated in the Summer Campaign, sailed on the ships, spent two years in short-term missions in one of the OM fields, who caught the vision and never looked back.

All this has been possible because some people took a risk.

Chapter Ten

They Died

*'Don't let anyone look down on you because you
are young, but set an example for the believers in
speech, in life, in love, in faith and in purity.'*
1 Timothy 4:12

Youth has its critics. Having started in missions
at the age of twenty, I have always been a firm
believer in mobilising and involving youth in
missions.

I am familiar with the usual objections to
involving the young. I understand the concerns
of the older, wiser generation of Christians who
feel this way, but this does not mean I am in full
agreement with them. I have heard Christian
leaders speaking against the use of the young and
the inexperienced, emphasising that the New
Testament Church sent out only the best. I am
not sure that position is tenable.

God is not constrained by an individual's age
or experience, qualifications or gender. God uses

all kinds of people – young and old, experienced and inexperienced, the godly and the ungodly (check out the Old Testament on that one!), and men as well as beasts. If one ever gets carried away by the fact that God particularly uses them, perhaps the fact that God also used a donkey in His service should help them to stay humble.

The Bible shows us young people taking their place in the overall divine scheme – Joseph, Samuel, David and Josiah to name a few.

I have other reasons for believing that young people will play a significant role in missions in the new millennium. Enthusiasm and youthfulness are on their side and I rate their degree of adaptability and flexibility a lot higher than those of older people. They certainly have fewer commitments – like children, family and career. They also have more years of service ahead. They are generally healthier simply because the normal process of wear and tear has not set in. Being single or newly married, they have greater mobility. Having just completed university, college, or a stint in the working world, they bring some of the most relevant skills and expertise to today's missions.

I have worked with young people for as long as I have been involved in missions and have a high regard for them. I believe it is foolish to underestimate their contribution. I am convinced they can make an impact for Jesus Christ in this world.

In OM there have been many deaths in service. Many have died in action, killed while on the field serving the Lord. The majority was young – they received an early crown from the King whom they served and died for. OM in East Asia Pacific owes its growth to many people and to many things, but I believe it owes most to those who have laid down their lives in this region.

Karen Goldsworthy and Sofia Sigfridsson

In August 1991 my wife and I were eagerly awaiting the arrival of our second child. Someone called the OM Hong Kong office to ask if I knew about the attack on the *Doulos* in Zamboanga, Southern Philippines. Puzzled, I tuned in my radio to the BBC World Service to find out what had happened.

The incident had taken place the previous night at an international concert held onshore. More than a thousand people had packed into an auditorium to watch this concert by the *Doulos* staff and crew. As the concert came to a close, the speaker stood to end the evening with a Gospel message. Suddenly several men threw grenades into the hall.

A grenade landed near the lectern but failed to explode. A second grenade landed backstage where about sixty *Doulos* members were huddled together in silence, either praying for the audience or simply waiting for the final curtain call. The second grenade exploded in front of two young women who were praying. New Zealander, Karen, and Sofia, an Ethiopian from Sweden, were killed instantly. Both were only nineteen years old, Karen was a personal friend. About thirty *Doulos* staff were injured in the attack. When all of the casualties were brought back to the ship's main lounge that night it apparently resembled a field hospital after a bloody battle. Some injuries turned out to be permanent.

Let me refer to Elaine Rhoton's *The Doulos Story*, which describes that terrible night. In this book she quotes George Barathan, one of the ship leaders

When we arrived at Brent Hospital, we found a large crowd there already. No one seemed to be in charge to monitor the people, especially inside the wards where our patients were being treated. Joe was brought to a bed. I tried to go from bed to bed to visit, but there were too many local people, along with a few nurses, rushing here and there. It was hot and stuffy without adequate ventilation.

I was relieved to find Simon Slator, a six-foot *Doulos* deck-hand, helping at the hospital. 'Sofia is gone,' he told me.

I was deeply shocked! He took me to her room. Sitting with her was a Filipino brother, keeping watch and mourning. Anger mixed with sadness filled my heart. I kept asking, 'Lord, why did this happen?' After a few minutes I left the room with Simon. The Filipino brother remained.

While I was going around to see the patients once more, Simon came to me again and said, 'Karen is gone too.' In one corner of a ward I saw her lying on a bed with her eyes closed. There were a few people standing around her.

I felt then that I needed to get back to the ship soon and inform Bernd [the ship's director] about the two deaths.

I returned to *Doulos* and as I walked through the main lounge, I saw the ship's staff praying in many parts of the main lounge and port lounge. Bernd was at the front, with Chacko [the assistant director] standing a bit further away. I broke the news to Bernd about the deaths of Sofia and Karen. He immediately turned away and broke down in tears. I sat beside him on one of the chairs and put my arm around his shoulders to comfort him. Soon Chacko joined us and he too was deeply disturbed by the news.

Five minutes later, Bernd got up to announce the news of the deaths. As Bernd mentioned the home-going of each person, the ship staff began to cry, hugging one another for comfort. It was a very moving sight for me. After a little while, people began praying together in small groups. Chacko took much of the responsibility to lead the people in prayer. He was a great strength to Bernd during those difficult hours.[1]

My immediate response on hearing the terrible news was to telephone Bernd in Zamboanga. Bernd and I had worked on board together the year before and had become close friends. I offered to fly to Manila to give whatever help I could. Under the sponsorship of the OM Hong Kong board I flew down to meet the injured and the dead who were being flown up from Zamboanga. Upon arrival in Manila I teamed up with Peter Maiden, OM's Associate International Director, and Dale Rhoton, General Director of the Ship Ministry, and we launched straight into pastoral care at the hospital where the *Doulos* people were being cared for.

There were about thirty in the hospital. Peter, Dale and I set about visiting each injured person. The worst was over for some but others were still undergoing surgery. Chi Kong, the cook on board who had escaped from China several years before and since become a German permanent resident, was unable to respond – tubes were fed through his throat to suck out the phlegm and feed him the liquid he needed. Surprisingly everyone was in good spirits. Kelly Inae, from Papua New Guinea, was as usual beaming from ear to ear despite the injury to his leg, which has left a permanent limp. All were more concerned for others still on the ship than themselves.

The next day, Peter suggested serving communion round the hospital beds. We started our rounds, one of us reading from Scripture, one of us praying and another serving communion. It was good to keep our focus, through the communion, on Jesus.

It took several weeks for the worst to be over. The bodies of Karen and Sofia were flown back to their respective countries.

This incident is forever etched in my memory. It serves as a challenge to expect risk, perhaps even death, as we give our lives and our time to God. It also serves as a challenge to commitment. It reminds me not to disregard the service of young people as insignificant.

Karen became a friend of my family when we were on board. A brief account of her testimony just before her death brought me much encouragement. She wrote

There have been many hard times where God has been at work moulding and shaping me. Before leaving for this A-team, life was difficult for me. Everything seemed to be going wrong and I was hurting. I did a lot of crying but I made a big mistake by not crying out to God. I tried to sort things out in my own strength. The night before we left the ship, I realized I couldn't go on as I was. I was just getting into a mess. I spent time till early in the morning talking, crying and praying with a friend. I left one prayer request with her: that while on A-team I would see God in a new way and regain my first love for him.

We arrived here and began our programme. I was involved and doing my part, but my heart wasn't in it. I felt God was a long way away. At many of the meetings there was praise and worship but I couldn't worship. There was an uncomfortable barrier between God and myself – my pride and stubbornness. As the first week went on, I tried to ignore the emptiness, the restlessness I was feeling in my heart, but I could see all around me Christians who had great joy and an obvious love for the Lord. I realized I needed to get right with God! I finally gave in, handed over my burdens to the Lord, and came back into his waiting arms. Then what a *joy* it was to go out on meetings! I *enjoyed* the times of praise and worship with churches. God is so loving and forgiving. The first week I had felt so alone; it was good to turn around and go running back to my father's arms![2]

Abel Ventura

Abel was from Mexico. In 1978 he was on the MV *Logos*. Just before I left to go to Taiwan from Okinawa, Abel came to my cabin. He wanted someone to pray with him. Earlier I had become a good friend of his predecessor, Samuel Castro, from whom I had learned some Spanish. I had been practising my limited phrases on Abel and he had taken a liking to me. He expressed his deep desire to glorify Jesus in his life, and I remember very clearly Abel's prayer – it was one of complete commitment, of total surrender to the Lord. He had a burden for missions and he wanted to dedicate his life for that purpose. I left the following day for Taiwan and never saw him again.

After my preparation work for the MV *Logos* in Taiwan I returned to Singapore. Several weeks later, the MV *Logos* arrived in Taiwan. It was towards the end of the stay that the accident happened. Abel went with a *Logos* team to the beach for a swim. Whether it was a strong current that pulled him away, or whether Abel hit his head on the rock, no one was sure. Herbert, a burly German, saw Abel struggling and dived in to save him. But by the time he was pulled from the water he was dead.

When the telex message came to me in Singapore I was terribly shocked. It seemed so unreal. I remember going to my room where I knelt down and broke down before the Lord. I prayed a prayer of thanksgiving that Abel was now with Him, and I prayed for Abel's family in Mexico. I also re-dedicated my life to the Lord.

A service was held for Abel and his body was flown back to Mexico. Abel was in his mid-twenties. Praise God that he is now with Him. We have not seen many Mexicans moving out in missions in OM, perhaps they are with other mission groups, but I wonder if there are many whose prayers were of the depth that Abel prayed.

Prisca Ahn

Prisca, a Korean woman in her early thirties, was with the MV *Doulos* in Bombay in 1987. She was out on an errand when death took her. Bombay public buses do not wait for passengers, commuters are supposed to run after the bus and board while it is still in motion. Passengers had to hit the road running when alighting as well. Prisca, being new to India, was not used to this practice. She missed her step, lost her balance, and fell. She sustained head injuries and for the next few days was in intensive care in the hospital. She died without regaining consciousness.

Her family in Korea asked that her body be cremated. Dr Allan Adams, then Director of the MV *Doulos*, and several Korean leaders carried the ashes back to Korea. Her family was devastated.

Maritess

Maritess, or Tess as we called her, was a petite Filipina from Cagayan De Oro, Philippines. Despite her size she possessed a very strong will.

It was this strength of will that saw her serving on board the *Doulos* as the Accommodation Department team leader. Unfortunately she had to return home when she was diagnosed with Raynauds Disease – a rare vascular disorder. Undaunted by her condition, she established the OM office in her hometown of Cagayan De Oro.

Tess once shared, 'I want to go to Uzbekistan. I want to serve the Uzbeks before God will take me home. I know that the Lord will bring me home whether I stay or go. I want to go.' Sheer determination saw her arrive in Uzbekistan shortly after this.

Nine months into her service in Uzbekistan Tess' illness returned forcing a premature return to the Philippines. Within two weeks of her return, she was desperately ill in Maria Reyna Hospital. She died shortly afterwards. She left only three things she could call her own – a memory book that contained a collection of thoughts from friends about her, a map of Uzbekistan and a Uzbek hat.

Al Nueva, who was cook on *Logos* when I was a trainee, but now the Principal of a Seminary, prayed this prayer at Tess' funeral: 'Lord, thank you for the life of Maritess who became an example for all of us. Her death brought us to a time of reflection about our own walk with you. She exemplified an uncompromising faith until the end.'

Byoung Soo Son

In July 1997 I visited the MV *Doulos* in Port Moresby. Halfway through my stay on board I received a telephone call from Peter Maiden in the UK, and moments later, from Joseph Lee, Director of OM Korea, informing me of the sudden death of a Korean brother named Byoung Soo Son in Ashgabad, Turkmenistan. A fax message confirmed the news

> Today, July 28th, the group in Ashgabad went sharing and swimming in Lake Ashgabad. About noon, as they were in the water, Byoung Soo went out from the more shallow area. Nothing special was going on when he suddenly cried out, 'Help me, help me'. After that he disappeared and did not rear his head again. The team could not find him for about an hour. When they did, Byoung Soo was already dead.

In a crisis like this, I feel it is important to be with the OM leader concerned to offer support and advice. My offer to Joseph to be where he wanted me to be was readily accepted.

The plan was for me to fly directly to Seoul, Korea, to await the arrival of the ashes. This plan, however, was changed when we found out that Turkmenistan did not have cremation facilities. All the dead are buried there.

Byoung Soo's family asked that we make burial arrangements and then send them a video of the funeral. The funeral was set for the following Monday. It was Wednesday when Joseph and I agreed to make our way to Ashgabad. I arrived on Thursday in Singapore and quickly obtained an invitation letter from Ashgabad that would get me a visa upon arrival. It seemed miraculous that the fax got through to me in the middle of the night in Singapore from a place only several days ago I did not even know existed! Another provision from the Lord was a seat on a flight to Istanbul, Turkey, from where I could catch a connection to Ashgabad. The plane was fully booked both ways.

My colleague Bertil Engqvist, Area Co-ordinator of OM West and Central Asia and I stayed with friends in Istanbul. We took a mid-night flight on Sunday night, planning to arrive in time to attend the funeral on the Monday afternoon. Bertil still did not have his invitation letter in hand when we landed in Ashgabad. He was held up for several more hours at the airport checkpoint before he was released.

In its architecture and design Ashgabad is like many cites built by the Soviets. The Turkmen resemble Middle Easterners. In summer the temperature soars, Ashgabad was 40 degrees centigrade when I arrived. I was fortunate the temperature the previous week had been 45 degrees centigrade. The first thing I noticed upon stepping into the team house was the melted candle on the dining table.

When we arrived at the team house several other OM representatives were already there. From Korea were Joseph Lee, Elder Bae (a member of OM Korea board), and Byoung Soo's spiritual father who was also his closest friend. Daniel St John, Byoung Soo's Field Director, came from another Central Asian State, and Jae Han, another Korean leader living in West Asia, was also there.

One hundred and fifty Russian and Turkmen friends that Byoung Soo had made in the two years there joined us at the funeral. The service was held in the main hall in a village where Byoung Soo and the team had concentrated their mission efforts. The grief and genuine sorrow among those who came was evident. Byoung Soo's body was placed in a velvet casket with the national flags of Turkmenistan and Korea displayed close by. Many old folks from the Home of the Elderly came to the service, while he was alive Byoung Soo had brought them joy and laughter, his death had now brought them immense pain and sorrow.

The service was simple – Daniel led it while Joseph and Bertil brought hope and encouragement from the God whom Byoung Soo had served, and with whom he is now spending eternity. Several close friends from different parts of the world acted as pall-bearers.

The burial site belonged to the Orthodox Church. It was a miracle that a permit had been obtained just hours before to bury Byoung Soo there. As the casket was lowered, the group of Russian believers sang some familiar hymns in Russian. The person in charge of the proceedings asked me to say a prayer. It was a huge privilege to pray for someone that I considered a young hero. At the end of my prayer, I pronounced in no uncertain terms, that 'Jesus is the Resurrection and the Life.' These were the same words that are now inscribed on Byoung Soo's marble gravestone, in Turkmen, English and Korean.

Many went on camera to pay tribute to Byoung Soo. He had left a deep impact on their lives and they wanted his family and church in Korea to know this. 'Byoung Soo is the first person taken to glory since we started work in Central Asia in 1990,' Daniel St John said later.

After the funeral we rested in the shade of the grapevine in the courtyard of the team house. There was a knock on the metal door at the gate, three heads peered in, all Korean. One of them asked, 'Is Byoung Soo in?' Imagine their utter shock when we told them we had just returned from his funeral. They had come to discuss with Byoung Soo an outreach effort they were planning for the following spring. Byoung Soo had been corresponding with them and was looking forward to the partnership in the Gospel.

Byoung Soo had been planning to go home to Korea at the end of the summer. Now he had gone to his real home. He was only twenty-nine. 'Precious in the sight of the Lord is the death of his saints' (Ps. 116:15).

These were the young ones who have gone on ahead of us. They died. In their place I believe that more people will rise to take up the baton and continue the race.

---

[1] Rhoton, E. (1997). *The Doulos Story*, Carlisle: OM Publishing, p. 360–361.

[2] Rhoton, E. (1997). *The Doulos Story*, Carlisle: OM Publishing, p. 378.

Chapter Eleven

Fragrant Harbour

*'. . . and you will be my witnesses in Jerusalem,
and in all Judea and Samaria, and to the ends
of the earth.'*
Acts 1:8

In October 1990, Irene, Justin, only two years old
at that time, and I moved to the Pearl of the
Orient, Hong Kong. I wanted to help in establishing the ministry in Hong Kong before China
resumed sovereignty over the territory. I was also
to explore the possibility of ministry involvement
in East and North-East Asia.

At that time Stella Chan, a dynamic visionary,
was leading our work there. We conducted a
'Love Hong Kong' campaign in 1991, mobilising
young people, mainly in teams, to work with
local churches in Hong Kong. For the next two
years a small team of us went about sharing
and preaching on missions in the territory's
churches. We operated from a tiny office at the

Youth for Christ premises in Canton Road, Kowloon. Elvin, Alan, Ruth and I squeezed into this confined space each day. On two occasions an additional three people joined us from the MV *Doulos* to prepare for the visit of the ship to Hong Kong. Thankfully an adjacent room was made available.

We would take turns to go down to the street below and buy snacks – 'pows' (Chinese hamburgers), stewed cuttlefish, black sauce pig's ear, or the Cantonese delicacy, chicken feet – we enjoyed them all!

We had to move to another tiny office next to the notorious Temple Street. At night Temple Street comes alive with shops and stalls, patronised by locals and tourists, it is also renowned for the flesh trade. Mama-san (old ladies, usually), are posted at the foot of narrow stairways, urging the imprudent to enter for a fleeting moment of pleasure. Temple Street also boasts a string of gambling houses and illegal street hawkers. The most encouraging sight for me was to see the few neon-lit crosses that shone above the stalls; they belonged to several small churches. For the more cautious Christian Temple Street is out of bounds, but it became one of the many places our family liked to take visitors to.

Moving from office to office was very disruptive, every move made resulted in some loss of ministry partners, friends and contacts. An office of our own would have been an ideal solution but in land-scarce Hong Kong property prices were exorbitant.

Several months later Stella brought a man to my flat. This man's father had just died and had willed a percentage of his legacy to charitable organisations (OM is registered under this category). He gave Stella and I a cheque for 1.5 million Hong Kong dollars, enough to buy a flat. I had never received such a big gift to OM before. To say that Stella and I were delighted was an understatement – we were delirious! God had provided way beyond our imagination.

In due course OM Hong Kong bought a flat on Cameron Road, in the heart of Tsim Sha Tsui, Kowloon, which was renovated and transformed into an office. The office continues to be a reminder of the way the Lord provided so tangibly.

The property market is one of the main industries that drive the former British colony. Irene and I had to hunt around for a reasonably priced flat. For nine months we lived on Prince Edward Road and enjoyed the nearby markets and eating-places. We attended the Kowloon Tong CMA Church on Waterloo Road. At one end of Prince Edward Road was Kai Tak Airport. As we lived right under the flight path for the approach to the airport we got used to the roar of aeroplanes skimming the rooftops above us. We were told that should an aircraft ever crash down on to Kowloon City tens of thousands of lives in the area would be lost. This shows how compact living conditions were. Thankfully such a disaster never occurred while Kai Tak was open. It was closed in 1998 and replaced by the brand-new Hong Kong International Airport in Chek Lap Kok.

One of my favourite haunts was the Walled City. By then most of the residents had moved out, leaving only the shops and dental clinics along the fringes. Eventually even they would be evicted to make way for a park and a modern shopping centre. Whereas one would not dare to venture into the City during its heyday – even police entered in groups – I was quite safe going in alone.

The Walled City, structurally, was a disaster waiting to happen. Extra rooms, floors, illegal structures, had been haphazardly and irresponsibly added on to the original blocks to provide more space. I walked through the maze of darkened alleys and corridors, deserted but for the illegal hawkers preparing their unhygienic food for their unlicensed stalls. At one point no less than 200 unlicensed dentists were operating from here. But one look at the remaining dental clinics with their modern equipment dispelled the notion that they were fly-by-night set-ups. I got the impression that they knew their job.

Our next home was in Fan-ling, just two stops from the Chinese border on the MTR train line.

It took an hour from there to get into Kowloon. We remember our time in Fan-ling as two of the happiest years of our family life. The setting was rural, though we lived right in the middle of Luen Wo Market – a standard stop for tourists. We enrolled Justin in a Cantonese kindergarten and soon he was jabbering in the language. Our second child was on the way, Marianne was born several months later in Hong Kong.

I am basically a survivor. When I find myself in a new situation I adapt by discovering the way the locals go about doing and obtaining things. My knowledge of a little Cantonese helped. At Luen Wo Market farmers from around the district sold fresh, cheap produce. We also became regulars at the local eating-places. I soon bought a bicycle and explored the surrounding area together with Justin who was strapped into a safety seat on the back.

A Gurkha barracks was located in the nearby countryside. I would often cycle there and into their rifle firing range. If no red flag was displayed one could cycle right to the target area. From there I would either hike or run up the hills. At the top was barbed wire marking the restricted zone separating the New Territories from China. From a distance one could see the Chinese mainland, or rather the booming border city of Shenzhen. At other times I would go on a two-hour circuit ride which covered some of the most beautiful countryside in Hong Kong. One time I carried Justin, then four years old, on this circuit. It took me four hours. I staggered home exhausted.

Our third move was to Aberdeen, located on the south-western corner of Hong Kong Island. Transliterated from Cantonese, it is 'Little Hong Kong'. We moved because Justin's new school was on Hong Kong Island. Aberdeen is a satellite town surrounded by steep hills on three sides and the sea on one. The harbour used to be the place the Boat People laid up their Chinese junk boats, during the occasional typhoons it was a safe shelter for them. There is a free boat ride for all patrons to the Jumbo Restaurant – a floating restaurant designed like a palace. This became our favourite restaurant for taking friends and relatives to; the lunchtime 'tim-sum' was modestly priced. Marianne started Cantonese kindergarten in Aberdeen. With two children we were kept busy. I enjoyed taking them up to the hill where the reservoir was located, a good two-hour hike through nature.

There are more than a thousand churches in Hong Kong. Major denominations operate schools, educational institutions, hospitals, hotels, homes for the aged, blind and disabled, and a range of other welfare services. Because of the return to China in 1997, many pastors and church leaders had already migrated, and more were expected to follow. The need for replacements was acute. Almost every other Sunday I was speaking in churches and never failed to notice the need for pastoral workers. The handful of Bible colleges was training future workers but the demand was far greater than the supply.

The Chinese churches, in Hong Kong, Taiwan and in the Asian region, have a tendency towards ethnocentrism. In missions terms Chinese churches tend to send workers to work among the Chinese in other places. At conferences and conventions there have been efforts to broaden the missions vision of the Chinese church to go beyond missions to the Chinese. It is still early days but we hope for a flood of workers from the Chinese churches carrying the Gospel across to other cultures.

It is an encouragement to see individuals, couples and groups sent out by the Hong Kong churches for outreach with OM in Western Europe, Eastern Europe, North Africa, the Middle East, Central Asia and South Asia. A good number, mostly women, have chosen to continue long-term in OM. Sue, for instance, had served in East Africa for almost ten years, Ying and Mei, in North Africa, and Maureen, in France.

Maureen was an English teacher in a pres-tigious school in Hong Kong before she left for France to study theology there. In a few years Maureen was fluent in French as well as English and Cantonese. After graduation she joined OM in the mid-1980s and lived in Paris. She was the administrator of OM France and took on responsibility in the training department as well. Blessed with many abilities, Maureen has just been appointed the Associate Field Leader of OM France, so proving that Hong Kong Christians do have staying power in cross-cultural missions.

Since I left in December 1994, the work in Hong Kong under Stella has grown. It now has a New Immigrant Ministry, focusing on the immigrants coming out of China, at a rate of 150 per day. Many of these mainlanders need help in adjusting to Hong Kong. A wealthy lady offered a shophouse in the prestigious Midlevels, on Hong Kong Island, at a rent of 1 Hong Kong dollar per year for the next five years, for our use. It is now a centre offering help to new immigrants. We long for the day when we can channel Christians from the Chinese churches in China into other parts of the world. We may not have long to wait!

Chapter Twelve

Land of Genghis Khan

*'. . . and on this rock I will build my church, and
the gates of Hades will not overcome it.'*
Matthew 16:18

What are Mongolians like?

In Cantonese movies I had seen Mongolians
were depicted as a fierce and warlike people
with hats made from fox fur and great skill on
horseback. Besides these images I vaguely
remembered the stories of Genghis Khan and his
grandson Kublai Khan. As a child I drew pictures
of Genghis Khan on my drawing block, copied
from my history textbook.

I began praying for Mongolia in the late 1970s
having learned that there was no official church
in Mongolia as it was under Communist rule. At
that time there was no more than a handful of
believers in the entire country. In 1990, after 70
years of Communism, the country adopted
democracy. If there was a hope that the new form

of government would reverse the slide to economic chaos and hardship, it quickly dissipated. The old system had been too entrenched. It would be a long haul to see this landlocked country restored to its former glory.

Noeh Vios, a Filipino who joined OM in the early 1980s, had been praying for Mongolia for a long time. When he married Sally, a neurologist, practising and lecturing at the Philippine University, they sensed the call to go to Mongolia. After several years of prayer and preparation, they arrived in Ulaan Baatar, the capital of Mongolia, in September 1991. Noeh would teach English at the local school and Sally would be a medical consultant with a service organisation. Hezron, their young son, followed them. It was my duty as their Field Leader to provide the care that they needed, which meant I had to make a pastoral visit to them.

I had never imagined that I would visit Mongolia one day. To avoid the harsh winter I chose to visit in October. I left Hong Kong at a temperature of 30 degrees centigrade, and I arrived in –14 degrees centigrade weather in Ulaan Baatar, a difference of 44 degrees centigrade! I had taken warm clothes but soon discovered that these were grossly inadequate. It was freezing. One night as I was travelling in a Land Rover the temperature hit –20 degrees centigrade, the coldest I had ever experienced. Noeh informed me that the temperature drops to –48 degrees centigrade in the country over the winter, freezing to death a number of livestock. The Mongolian winter lasts nine months, leaving only three short months for summer!

All my visits have been pre-winter or post-winter, so the Mongolia I have seen was bleak. Most visitors come during the summer when the green grass appears to replace the dull winter brown and the leaves are on the trees. In summer everyone is out on the street enjoying the warmth. It is the time to engage in the three popular Mongolian sports – riding, wrestling and archery. The gentle steppes over much of Mongolia offer a natural terrain for marathon horse races or relays, which may stretch up to 20 kilometres in distance.

A visit to Mongolia must include a visit, if not a stay in a Ger – a Mongolian traditional tent. These are almost circular in design, with sections of flat walls forming the round structure. The wealthier the owner is the more sides there are. A Ger belonging to the average family will have six sides, forming a hexagon. In the middle of the tent is a hole in the roof, which provides ventilation and light. A cauldron of lamb stew or soup is always available. As lamb is the most common meat guests are offered this meat with some noodles thrown in. Modern Gers in the city may even have a television set and a telephone. City Gers have an outside hut that is used as a toilet. In the country they don't worry about such luxuries.

What do couples do for privacy when the Ger is such a communal structure? I was told that some might hoist a flag at the doorway to warn off indiscreet intruders. Mongolians like to move to the city to their Russian-built flats during winter to escape the cold. Gers in the country are like summer homes.

The Mongolian barbecue is famous throughout the world. I have seen many variations cooked outside Mongolia but never tasted one that comes close to the real thing. I remember a group of us having a picnic next to a river that was frozen solid. Pork was used instead of the normal lamb – a sheep is usually slaughtered for the meat. Stones of different shapes and sizes were placed on the fire and left to heat up. The cook then placed the meat in a container that looked like a milk can. Onions, carrots, potatoes, salt and pepper were added. Next the stones were transferred into the container and it was sealed tight. For several minutes the hot stones cooked the concoction inside the container. The container was then shaken and rolled on the ground to mix up the ingredients. This done it was ready to serve.

In 1992 Mongolia was just two years into democracy and in dire straits financially. The Russians who had supplied all that they needed and enjoyed now had survival problems of their own and Mongolia was left out on a limb. This was exacerbated by the geography of the country – landlocked and inaccessible. The nearest ports were in Russia or China, a neighbour she was still not quite ready or willing to associate with after a history of humiliation. Japan and Korea were the main aid-givers but aid was proving to be inadequate. The once crowded shops filled with Russian vodka and goods were now nearly empty. I am told that the situation has now improved a little.

When the country adopted democracy Christians from around the world made their way there. In just two years the number of Mongolian Christians grew to several hundred. Four fellowships were established in Ulaan Baatar, the capital, and several in Darkhan and Edernet. Today the number of Mongolian Christians is estimated to be anything between 5,000 to 10,000. Ulaan Baatar alone has 30 or more churches. Relatively speaking this country probably has the fastest-growing church anywhere in the world. It is exciting what God is doing after so many years of prayer.

The Mongolian church is a young church. Many of the converts were either teenagers or young adults. For a time, very few older Mongolians were interested in the Gospel. Young Mongolians therefore led the churches – several I met were in their early twenties.

Noeh suggested to me the idea of taking some Mongolians with us on the MV *Doulos* to provide them with training. Our motivation was to introduce the Mongolian church to missions, to encourage them to look outwards and not to be self-absorbed. We had concerns – would we prematurely expose them to a lifestyle that might be detrimental to their growth? Would we set a wrong precedent? Would we give the wrong impression? Finally we decided to take two Mongolians on a trial basis. They would need to speak some English, be sent and recommended by their home church, and must return home after the training. Furthermore they must be sponsored.

The last condition was the easiest. Friends in Hong Kong and Singapore were very happy to help financially. Two young Mongolian men were screened – Bayar and Bat. Both went on to spend two profitable years on the MV *Doulos* around East Asia. Both returned to Mongolia. Bat met a German girl on the ship, later they were married and they now live in Darkhan where Bat, a gifted musician, is leading a church. They have a daughter. Bayar returned home to continue his university studies, and recently graduated with a degree in Economics. He now works in the finance department of World Vision, Mongolia, developing their micro-business projects within the country with the aim of assisting Mongolians in self-sustaining businesses.

The next two were Javkhlan and Brian.
Javkhlan was the first Mongolian deckman on
the *Doulos* and probably the first Mongolian
seaman ever – remember Mongolia has no sea
and therefore no seamen! He returned to
Mongolia to take over the pastoral duties of a
church in the outskirts of Ulaan Baatar from a
Korean pastor. Javkhlan, Bat and Bayar were a
credit to their OM training. The fact that they
were in demand by other agencies indicated that
the training on the ship was profitable. But we
also had our first casualty.

Everyone who pictured Mongolians as in-
expressive and unsmiling would change their
mind when they met Brian (not his real name).
Brian was a young, extrovert and likeable fellow.
He worked in the book exhibition and became a
member of the creative team on board.

At first no one noticed the subtle change in
Brian's lifestyle. His dressing became stylish and
his collection of music compact discs grew. No
one asked where he got the money from and no
one suspected theft. When the book exhibition
reported to the Captain a substantial amount of
money unaccounted for from the day's sale of
books Brian was a suspect because the money
disappeared during his shift duty. On further
investigation the amount unaccounted for was
found in Brian's locker.

Brian was spared the charge of having committed a crime. As he was coming to the end of

his two-year commitment anyway it was agreed
that he should leave. After explaining to the ship
family, Brian left the ship in shame, but not
without love and assurance. We heard that Brian
worked for some time in Korea before returning
to Mongolia, where he is trying to make a living.
The other Ex-*Doulos* brothers provide the
periodical fellowship and friendship that he
needs.

Odno and Oyuuna were the first Mongolian
ladies who trained with us. Both had a positive
time on the ship. Odno returned to Mongolia
with the desire to study law, which she does in
the evening while working at World Vision,
Mongolia in the day. Oyuuna is involved in her
church.

In their second year in Ulaan Baatar Noeh and
Sally joined an outfit called JCS International.
Under their leadership, OM became a member
of JCS International. This is a consortium made
up of 16 or more Christian organisations,
which is recognised by the government. People
sent out by the member bodies work under
the supervision of JCS International. Its main
purpose is to provide expertise and assistance in
aid and development to the people of Mongolia.
Staff of JCS International are involved in
veterinary projects, cattle projects, agricultural
assistance and so on. Lately they have been able
to channel people into institutions and kinder-
gartens as teachers and administrators.

Alcohol abuse has been a problem throughout Mongolia's history. Kublai Khan died of alcoholism in the fourteenth century. With the coming of democracy alcohol laws put in place under Communism were no longer enforced.

It was dismaying to see the social problems caused by alcoholism. Due to this and unemployment child abuse had increased. To escape abuse many children ran away from home making their way to the capital, only to find that life there was no better. The abuse continued. Several hundred of them made the city sewer tunnels their home in an attempt to keep warm in winter.

Under JCS International's Alcohol Abuse Reduction Project, Sally and her team began an alcohol abuse prevention programme educating schoolchildren about the evils and effects of alcohol and taking alcoholics through a recovery programme. The project was featured on Mongolian television with an interview segment with Sally.

Noeh and Sally are now based in Manila. Three young women – Enerbelle and Cynthia from the Philippines, and Marcela from the Czech Republic, are serving with OM in Mongolia. There have been requests to send Mongolians to the *Doulos* for training. We will continue to play our part, albeit small, in expanding God's kingdom in Mongolia.

Several years ago, Steve Hart, retired OM accountant, sent me this article

She held such promise! A girl from Mongolia, aged nineteen or twenty, recruited in London in 1973! She was born in Mongolia, had lived in France before moving to London, and spoke those three languages. We knew her by her English name Nelly.

She joined OM that summer, eager for training in missions. Her goal: to take the gospel back to her native Mongolia! That ancient grassy and desert land. Our hearts thrilled with Nelly: she might be God's instrument to bring Christ to that nation! So with the summer campaign finished, she signed up with OM France for her 1973 year-programme of training.

Sadly, it was not to be. She did not even get to the French town where she was going to serve. As she and her new team headed toward it, their van was in a smash-up. Nelly died at the scene. I attended the funeral in London. Part of it was in French – because Nelly's mother spoke no English. I visited with the mother afterward, and with the family Nelly had lived with in England.

Apart from the sorrow we shared, we all struggled with the devastating questions: Since Nelly was the only potential Mongolian missionary we knew, how could God allow her to be snatched from us? Now, who could take her place, and carry Christ to that land, which in 1973 was closed to foreign missionaries?

Steve found the answer in reports I wrote about what God was doing in Mongolia. He continues

Nelly died 21 years ago. These young men (who served on the ship) were born somewhere around that time. Could it possibly be that the Lord brought them into the world and to salvation in answer to Nelly's prayers for her homeland?

Only eternity will tell.

Chapter Thirteen

Feeling like a Chinese Sage

'... Our hope is that, as your faith continues to grow, our area of activity among you will greatly expand, so that we can preach the gospel in the regions beyond you. For we do not want to boast about work already done in another man's territory.'
2 Corinthians 10:15–16

Why does China hold such a fascination for so many people?

It was the dream of my parents' generation to see 'The Middle Kingdom' at least once in their lifetime, even better if they could spend the twilight years of their lives in their home village or ancestral town. My father came over to Singapore as a refugee in the early part of the twentieth century to find work and died without ever returning to his home of Ningpo, near Shanghai. My mother was born in Singapore and died in Singapore. She had harboured the desire to visit China but the country was then closed to outsiders. Also travel at that time was expensive, a luxury only the rich could afford.

We live in a different day and age. Before my son was six years old he had visited China four times – each time for a short and enjoyable holiday! If his grandparents were alive, they would be envious.

Some Chinese people visiting China for the first time have told me that the experience was like locating their ancestral or cultural roots. Others, perhaps with their subconscious mind already conditioned and fed with information and images from books, movies and television, said that they felt that they had been there before. Still others say that they felt an element of danger and risk. Perhaps this last group of people have read too many stories and imagine that they are still in the era of the forbidden Bamboo Curtain. In some sense, whatever one feels about China has a certain degree of possibility, simply because it is such a big country with such a big population – in fact the largest in the world. How one feels and what one discovers will probably hold true, somewhere, someplace in China.

How did I feel when I first entered China? As I knew that I would be revisiting the country in the future I simply went as a tourist and did some of the things that tourists do, although much of my time and energy were given to friends working or studying there. I treated China like any other country – with respect, with curiosity and, I trust, with enough sensitivity. This approach has served me well in my travels.

God has been working marvellously in China. Amazing accounts of believers shining in their faith amidst persecution are inspiring and motivating. Here again, whatever you have read or heard about the Chinese church is probably true, simply because it is so varied. If you were told of pressure and persecution in a certain province, it is true. If you read a report that another province enjoys the goodwill and favour of local officials, it is probably also true. There is great faith but there is also confusion caused by devious teachings and practices. But one thing can be confirmed – God is at work.

While there has been a mighty work of the Holy Spirit among the Chinese, one cannot say the same about the minority non-Chinese groups in China. There is some sign of outreach among them, but there is still a long way to go.

A tour of China with Bobby Chew, a colleague, proved memorable. Our purpose was to visit some friends and to see for ourselves what was happening in China. We flew from Singapore to Hong Kong, then took the train to Guangzhou. We then flew to Henan, Beijing, Xinjiang, Chengdu and Tibet before returning to Singapore via Chengdu and Hong Kong. In 16 days we visited seven cities and took nine flights plus a train ride. Two years later I went on a second trip, similar to the first, with another companion, young Peter Quak.

It was tiring but fun to travel with a companion. It cut out the loneliness and provided security and convenience. I returned from both trips with many stories to tell.

We perfected the art of queue-jumping at airport check-in counters. Let me assure you that this was a culturally acceptable thing to do. We arrived at the airport in good time for our flight from Beijing and obediently stood in the queue. Within an hour the two queues had swelled to eleven! That was when push came to shove. Bobby did a good job getting our boarding passes while I got our luggage checked through. Two years on, Peter and I were expecting the same chaos but were pleasantly surprised by the civility of everyone. Fewer people were travelling then as locals were now being asked to pay the same fares as foreigners.

Accommodation and food in China were reasonably cheap, especially so outside the main cities. We stayed in hotels. This may seem extravagant but in China hotels are modest rather than luxurious and most importantly, they are safe.

Food is economical if you are game for local fare and your stomach can cope with it. For the really adventurous there are all kinds of wild game served – bat, snake, lizard, fowl and much more. Restaurant operators are desperate for business and resort to heavy-handed means to obtain it. On a visit to Shenzhen with my family for the first time, we were pulled into a restaurant while walking along a popular food street. I ended up sustaining a scratch on my shoulder in a brief moment of indecision. Otherwise, my experience of China's food has been very pleasant indeed.

Food does affect morale. The OM food budget, especially on small land teams, was and still is small and balancing a missionary budget is often a very delicate exercise. So I found it a form of ministry to take people out for meals. Having a meal together provides an informal opportunity to talk and build relationships and friendships.

It was over meals that we learned about what God was doing through some of our friends in China. Most were there on student visas learning the Chinese language, Mandarin, or one of the minority languages in China. It is commendable and inspiring to see non-Asians tackling Mandarin. It isn't at all easy. Interestingly, some of the non-Asian friends I am associated with are able to speak the minority languages better than most of the Chinese, who, in the normal course of life and work, being the majority, have very little need or motivation to learn them. If study materials and teaching aids are the dire need of the Chinese church, then such needs for the minority believers can only be guessed at.

The establishment of the church among some of the minority groups is about 150 years behind the founding of the Chinese church. This may be due to historical suspicion and prejudice, lack of a cross-cultural focus in the church both inside and outside of China, and therefore the lack of committed workers, restrictions in terms of placement and visas, and the risks involved. Perhaps the Lord may bring about a breakthrough in the church among these groups. Then again breakthrough seldom comes unless there has first been blood, sweat, toil and tears.

In Xinjiang, the North-West Autonomous Province, there are 15 million people, half are Chinese, the other half are Uygurs, a group of people whose roots are Turkic. These people are nominal Muslims although only a small percentage actually practise. The Chinese government has an on-going programme of transmigration that involves transplanting groups of people, mainly the Chinese, to areas where the minority ethnic groups are found in large numbers. This move is political as well as social. There has been little love lost between the minority groups towards the dominant ethnic group, the Han Chinese. Hostilities stretch way back several centuries.

As far as I know there are only a few Uygur believers among the seven million plus population. Uygur scriptural materials are limited; the

New Testament is not even complete. However across the border in Kazakhstan there are several vibrant fellowships of Uygur believers. Some have been instrumental in helping and nurturing fellow-believers in China, not without risk of harassment. Discretion is the key to successful discipleship in such a place.

While winter can be harsh, it can also be beautiful. Normally a dusty and dry province, with the Taklamakan Desert in the middle, and the ring of population around this desert, the winter snow serves to cover all that is unpleasant to the eyes with its blanket of white. Unfortunately my visits always coincided with the mild seasons of May or October, when it is neither warm enough to be summer nor cold enough to be winter. What winter and snow I had seen in Xinjiang was in the pictures of travel books, except for the one time we went up to Tien Shan, or the Heavenly/Celestial Mountains. On a clear day, one could see the mountains from the capital, Urumqi.

Why I had not visited Tien Shan earlier still puzzles me. All visitors must, I was told, visit Tien Shan and Tien Chi, or the Heavenly Lake. I had been in Urumqi twice, and people found it odd that I had not been to these scenic spots. Tien Shan is two hours' drive from Urumqi. On my third visit I was determined to make the trip with Peter, my travelling companion. We made arrangements.

After an hour and a half drive to the foot of the mountains it took about half an hour for the steep climb to the top. The air became crisp and clear as the scenery fell back behind us. It was April, winter was coming to an end but summer had not yet arrived. So the view was still brown and drab, with pockets of green here and there. In summer it would have been breathtaking, although it was spectacular enough. We passed the Little Heavenly Lake on our way to *the* Heavenly Lake, which, together with the mountains, are the main attractions.

As we topped the crest the view that greeted us was hard to describe. The scenery reminded me of Switzerland with its mountains and lakes. It was beautiful and certainly deserved our attention. We took some time to drink it all in. The Heavenly Lake was still frozen, and in the distance we could see dots of people trudging across it, some on horseback. Someone pointed out the Tien Shan peak in the background.

The people who live up in the Tien Shan are Kazakhs. These mountain dwellers operate a thriving tourist industry, providing accommodation in traditional Yak, (not unlike the Mongolian Ger), and horse riding. Peter and I chose to try our hand at horse riding.

Our driver had informed us that an hour of horse riding would cost RenMinBi (RMB) 20, around 2.50 US dollars. We confirmed the price with the Kazakh horseman, and off we went, guided by the horseman. It was fun to ride on a horse, especially when one didn't know even the most basic skills. It was amazing to see how sure-footed the horses were. We rode up and down the slopes, and at one point even galloped. We had the time of our lives. After an hour and a half my backside was bruised and sore – testimony to my advancing age and condition. Peter, who is about sixteen years younger, hardly suffered at all!

When it was time to settle our horse riding bill the Kazakh horseman insisted we pay RMB200 per hour per horse, because we had been riding for an hour and a half he wanted RMB600. We nearly fell off our horses! Unfortunately it was his word against ours. The driver came to our rescue though. By rights we should have paid RMB60 for two horses, we paid RMB100 instead, including a handsome tip, even then the horseman wasn't happy. A lady who was travelling with us told us that she had only paid RMB10 for her ride so we really were swindled.

One week later in another part of China, horse riding was again offered to us, wisely we declined. Later we saw what happened to us re-enacted in another incident. But this victim was different – he created a scene. He shouted at the horseman for claiming RMB40 when RMB10 had been agreed (in Mandarin the two numbers sound similar). He wanted to make sure everyone else heard about it. We could only nod in agreement with him – like two Chinese sages who had gone through difficult life experiences.

Although we were not rude to our Kazakh horseman we certainly felt he was in the wrong. Without the knowledge of Jesus few would be truly honest in their dealings. We need to trust the Lord for the salvation of the Kazakhs this side of the border. Over in Kazakhstan, we had heard that the Lord had raised up several churches of Kazakh believers. Surely they hold one of the keys to reaching out to their own.

Another trip with Bob took us to Chengdu, the capital of Sichuan and the gateway city to Tibet, from where we flew to Lhasa. We had to pick up our tickets at one of the handful of tour agencies located at the Traffic Hotel. Before a ticket was issued a permit was needed; this came from Lhasa and had to be previously arranged.

The airport in Lhasa is 95 kilometres from the capital. The runway is carved out of a valley and surrounded on all sides by mountains. Lhasa is situated at approximately 3,700 metres above sea level and so all visitors are forewarned about high altitude sickness. We were advised to take medication to help us combat this but did not, partly because we had not wanted to go to the trouble of looking for an uncommon medicine, partly because we were confident that high altitude sickness would not affect us. We were mistaken.

On arrival at the hostel where we were staying I began to feel the first effects of high altitude sickness. The reception was on the second floor and our rooms were on the third. By the time I reached the reception with my rucksack on my back I was short of breath and panting heavily. I noticed that Bob was missing and went back to look for him. He was lying on the floor having blacked out from lack of oxygen. He was pale and his lips were white. We helped him up and he recovered well but after this incident we developed a healthy respect for high altitude sickness. We learned our lesson the hard way though, because we had not taken the recommended medication we suffered continuous headaches throughout the four days we were there.

The symptoms of high altitude sickness include feeling light-headed, shortness of breath and nausea. Both Bob and I suffered all three symptoms, but because I was the fitter one, I was still able to move around whilst Bob was forced to rest for much of the time. One afternoon I returned to the hostel room to find Bob breathing through a tube connected to a pillow. This was a bag of oxygen the Swiss hostel caretaker had bought for him from the shop for half a dollar. Bob offered me some. We were almost like addicts getting our fix!

Needless to say I made sure I took the necessary medication for my second visit to Tibet.

Except for some breathlessness I suffered very little else.

Tibet is often deemed to be Shangri-La – a land of mystical people and mythical beliefs high up in the mountains. In reality much tension exists between Tibet and the Chinese government. As in Xinjiang the government has moved Chinese people into Tibet. There are over five million Tibetans. Of these 1.5 million live in Tibet, the rest in other parts of China like Qinghai, Western Sichuan and Northwest Yunan. Over 100,000 Tibetans live in India, from which thousands have migrated to other countries.

Historically nearly every Tibetan family had at least one son entering monastic life. Recently a small percentage of families have been allowed to resume this practice. For centuries monastic life dominated Tibetan political, religious, educational and cultural life. Today monastic communities continue to influence Tibetan society. The search for enlightenment drives Tibetans to repetitiously perform merit-making acts, such as praying with the prayer wheel. With each revolution of the wheel, prayers are made to the heavens and thus gain merit for the believer. Keeping the butter lamps continuously lit is another important element of worship. Devout worshippers fully prostrate themselves by dropping to their knees and fully extending their bodies on the ground, several hundred times at a time.

There is good news and bad news about Tibet. The bad news is that relatively few Tibetans believe in Jesus. This is because few are exposed to the Gospel. At present there is no church in Tibet, only a handful of believers. In Nepal there are two fellowship groups. The good news is that God is establishing His Kingdom in the hearts of the Tibetan people. Never before has there been such opportunity to live and minister among the Tibetans. Unfortunately, not many are taking up this challenge. People are needed who are not only tough spiritually but physically as well. It has been said that to reach a Tibetan with the Gospel is like going into a lion's den to steal a cub.

Many foreigners take Tibetan language courses, attracted perhaps by what they know of Tibet, or by the Tibetan religion of Buddhism. It is not uncommon to see western Buddhists worshipping in the monasteries. John and Sue (not their real names) have lived in Tibet for several years. They found learning the language hard work in the beginning but are now effectively communicating in Tibetan and making many friends. Initially Tibet took them some getting used to. Even though they are both fond of sports and physically fit it took them several months to acclimatise to the high altitude. Thinking they were sufficiently acclimatised, they went for a jog. At sea level they could jog several kilometres, but they only managed 400 metres at 3,700 metres above sea level. They suffered body cramps due to lack of oxygen and took more than a week to recover. It was six months before they could enjoy a decent jog. If physical acclimatisation takes time, spiritual inroads will take much longer.

What happened to our high altitude sickness? As soon as we boarded our plane on the way out of Lhasa it disappeared as suddenly as it had arrived. By the time we touched down in Chengdu it had gone completely. This is why when mountaineering (not that I am an expert) as soon as one experiences high altitude sickness the solution is to descend. Chengdu was a descent of 3,700 metres.

The Tibetans, Uygurs and the Huis (Chinese Muslims) are amongst some of the greatest challenges to the church inside and outside of China. Will it be long before we see churches established among them? The Gospel came to China several hundred years ago, will we see a breakthrough soon?

Chapter Fourteen

Living in Indignity

*'And if anyone gives even a cup of cold water to
one of these little ones because he is my disciple,
I tell you the truth, he will certainly not lose
his reward.'*
Matthew 10:42

It came out of the blue.

'Hello, Rodney, Leong here. George Mueller called me from Germany to invite me to get a group of Singaporean doctors to join his group of German doctors for a medical camp in Hyderabad. What do you suggest I do?' asked Wei Leong, a good friend who was also a doctor in private practice.

One year ago I had introduced Leong to India. We went to Hyderabad, the capital of Andhra Pradesh in India. The headquarters of OM India are located in Secunderabad, the twin city of Hyderabad. Whilst in India Leong visited slums and held clinics for the poor under the auspices of OM's Good Shepherd Ministry. This ministry began ten years ago with the aim of bringing hope and dignity to the poor of India by providing medical care and education. Through this visit Leong had caught a vision that only doctors with a doctor's heart are able to catch. In the intervening year he had become friends with George Mueller.

George Mueller, a General Practitioner in Germany and Chairman of the OM Germany board, initiated the idea of a medical camp. At first it was an OM Germany/OM India project. With the involvement of Leong, OM Singapore made a late but welcome entrance. Leong managed to recruit three others to join the camp, these were Wee Shiong and David Tay who were both doctors and Charles Tan, a dentist.

The aim of the week-long camp in September 1998 was to vaccinate, examine and treat 10,000 people in the slums, especially children, as well as registering them for continued medical care.

Preparation for the camp was thorough. A committee headed by Saji John obtained permission, liaised with local authorities, village heads, the police and schools; organised logistics, transport, security, equipment and accommodation. Many volunteers were recruited. The team from Germany would bring equipment and two and a half tons of medicine and medical supplies. The state government had earlier given the necessary permission and its support to the project. With its medical emphasis the camp dovetailed nicely with the state's existing 'Health for All' programme.

An inauguration function was planned in Dundigal, a village 20 kilometres outside Secunderabad. When we arrived, more than a thousand people, men and women, boys and girls, were already gathered. The team became instant celebrities. Boys rushed up to shake hands with us. The cacophony of laughter, smiles, music, noise, conversations, announcements from the loudspeakers and shouts, made it a happy occasion for all.

The Health Minister of the State of Andhra Pradesh arrived to officiate at the launch of the camp. During the inauguration the Bible verse quoted at the opening of this chapter was read. A Christian man present was thrilled to hear the Bible read publicly in a village that was not known for anything Christian. The Minister of Health then welcomed the entire medical team made up of Germans, Indians and Singaporeans, and thanked us for making the effort and wished us well. On the last evening of the camp the Minister hosted an excellent dinner at a local club as an appreciation for the work done.

On the first day of the camp we returned to the place of the inauguration. The school had been transformed overnight by a group of workers into a makeshift hospital. A marquee was erected to receive all patients and queues quickly formed. After registration, each person was escorted to the respective room to see the team of doctors. Each team was made up of a doctor, an interpreter and an Indian medical staff or intern. A medical college had sent several of its graduates to help.

The steady stream of people began to build up as word got around the surrounding villages. The principal of the school we were using got all his students to come for the free treatment. Another school had the same idea and very quickly an extra queue was formed for children only. Several Indian doctors took on this new challenge screening the generally healthy children for signs of illness. By the end of the day approximately 1,800 people had been treated and the doctors were exhausted.

It was my job to organise the Rest and Recreation (R&R) for the Singaporeans in the group. Except for Leong, all were visiting India for the first time. I knew they had some preconceived ideas of India, and I wanted to show them another, more positive side of the people and country. We enjoyed a Rajasthani (Rajasthan is a north-western state) vegetarian buffet at a good local hotel. Leong told me that R&R was essential for retreat and refreshment before facing another hectic day.

By the third day, six of the doctors, including two Singaporeans, were sick, suffering from diarrhoea, fever and flu. Morale was low. The time of prayer and motivation in the morning before we set out was crucial in helping the team to focus on the job at hand. Once we entered the fourth day, the halfway point, the team seemed to have crossed a psychological hurdle. Morale rose again and the doctors were light-hearted with their patients. Among the doctors there was an exchange of knowledge and information. Germans and Singaporeans were more accustomed to the illness of the affluent like stress, hypertension and so on. The range of tropical illnesses that they were not normally exposed to intrigued them. David was delighted to try his hand at dentistry. It was in India that he pulled his first tooth!

Charles was pleased to be informed that the dental clinic was set up and ready for him and Manfred, another dentist, to use. On entering the 'clinic' he found a dentist's chair looking suspiciously like a barber's chair. This had been placed near the window in order to get more sunlight. The locations of the camp were without power and electricity and so a small generator was used. When more light was needed the dentists used torches. Manfred had acquired an entire set of dental equipment from various German institutions and planned to leave them in India when he left. In the week they were there hundreds of people were treated.

The camp changed location each day. Each time the composition of the crowd was different.

On the fifth day the camp went really basic – no buildings, just marquees. It was held next to the slums in Hyderabad.

An Indian slum is something to behold. There may be several hundred to several thousand dwellers in a slum, depending on the size of the plot of land. In many cases dwellers have arrived from the country seeking work in the city. Finding nowhere to stay they build makeshift shelters.

There are first, second and low-class slums. First-class slums are more organised – they have stronger, concrete houses, perhaps a school and some shops. Second-class slums are 'middle class'. Such classifications are of course relative. A visitor from an affluent society might well find even the second-class slums too much to bear.

Leong and I had had the privilege of visiting such a slum. Leong had spent the afternoon treating the sick – about seventy of them. When the clinic was over the slum elder invited us and the Good Shepherd team for a tour of the slum. We were amazed by its cleanliness. There was a well for communal use and the toilets, although offering little privacy, were constructed a distance away from the homes. Homes were built of mud, with thatched roofs. New arrivals erected theirs using branches for the roofs, plus cardboard and whatever plastic sheeting they could find. The slum leader pointed out a small piece of land that could be used as a classroom. On our tour we came across three 'ladies' talking. We found out they were 'eunuchs' – an Indian expression for transsexuals. They worked as dancers at functions and were often treated as outcasts.

A low-class slum is the worst imaginable. The conditions dwellers live in are absolutely appalling. One cannot imagine how human beings can live in such utter misery and indignity and yet they do. There is no power, no water – none of even the most basic of amenities. There are stray cats, dogs, pigs, goats, flies, mosquitoes and rubbish everywhere. The stench is revolting. I have yet to see someone who has come near a slum and not had their conscience troubled! As foreigners we were neither advised nor encouraged to venture near them. This was not only for our own security but also to avoid the perception that foreigners mean monetary benefits.

Testimonies from OM slum workers abound – some are heart-rending while others are heart-warming.

In the Kanpur slum (in Uttar Pradesh), Dayasagar shared the following story

A dirty child playing in filth is not an uncommon sight in the slums, where there is so much poverty. Children are often seen as a burden rather than a blessing. This is why there are so many abandoned children in the slums. One day, as Shakila was on her way out, she saw that a slum-child had fallen into a deep drain and was too exhausted to climb out by herself. Many people would have noticed this child earlier but no one bothered to help. In their eyes the child was no more valuable than a dying dog. But not to Shakila. She took compassion on the child, reached out into the filthy drain and pulled her out of it. Shakila brought the weak little girl home, washed her and watched over her until she was better. Then, she searched out the girl's grandmother and returned the girl to her only known, living relation.

The poor can be among the most generous of people. In Bhopal, Madhya Pradesh, the OM Good Shepherd school in the slum had to move eight times for lack of permanent premises. The situation was frustrating both for the teachers as well as the children. Building a school was out of the question as the team did not even have the resources to rent a hut for the school. One day, the grandmother of one of the children came to see Jacob, one of our workers. She said that her granddaughter, Kisan, had told her of the plight of the school and she wanted to help. She herself was a beggar and could not offer much in terms of money for the school. However she did have a hut and since she did not use it in the daytime, she offered the school the use of her simple home. Now the nursery classes for the slum children are conducted at this old woman's home!

An estimated 8,000 people were treated by the medicamp. The exercise of registering all the patients meant that Good Shepherd Ministry would have their records for any necessary follow-up treatment. Beyond meeting physical needs in a small way, we desire to see many of these people meeting Jesus Christ, the Divine Physician who can truly make them whole.

Joseph D'Souza, CEO of OM India, expressed his delight and gratitude for this opportunity to work together to serve the public. It had been especially busy for his staff, but the positive aspects of the effort far outweighed the minor problems experienced along the way. As a result of the camp OM India has been assured by the Minister of Health of his assistance and support in future endeavours, despite being a non-government organisation.

The German doctors shared how much their lives had been touched through contact with their Indian counterparts and patients. One dentist said he was very moved by the whimper of pain from a child when her tooth was extracted, and then to see her broad smile when the problem was removed.

The Singaporean doctors expressed similar sentiments. Wee Shiong had hugely appreciated the opportunity to serve the Lord when only a month ago he had thought service like this in his busy schedule was out of the question. David shared that his life was changed and given a new dimension. Charles, the most serious and quietest in the team, was thankful for this experience in using his skills for a good cause. And Leong, the ever-positive doctor, was over the moon that the medicamp had proved to be such a success.

On reflecting on my time spent in India over the years, four things come to mind. These are:

1. Friendship – lasting friendship, open friendship. I don't see my Indian colleagues every day as we work in different contexts, but I have always appreciated their friendship. This brand of friendship means, 'you first, don't worry about me'. Its essence is service.

2. Relationship – my colleague from the Middle East likes to say 'You have the watch, we have the time'. The Indian culture is like that, efficiency is not measured by punctuality. From Indians I am still learning about relating to others.

3. Life is fragile. The number of people in India is staggering and yet each represents someone made and loved by God. The sheer number of people makes the procreation and passing of life seem so mundane and fragile. Each of us has only one life. What makes mine different from the one in the slum is the location! We must learn not only to live and appreciate life, we must live it

for others. I always remember the day I nearly died from electrocution in India. In some sense it was in India that I got my life back.

4. A different perspective. We have our own sets of worries and pressures at home. Having met people who don't know where their next meal is coming from my worries seem relatively minor. India teaches me constantly to be contented with what I have. After a visit I don't easily get worried about the colour of my curtains, or the stain on the living room wall.

I recommend a visit to India to anyone, anytime.

Chapter Fifteen

Miraculous in the Monotonous

'. . . if you have faith as small as a mustard
seed . . .'
Matthew 17:20

Miracles often happen in the mundane.

When preparing a series of Christmas messages I came to the passage about the angels and
the shepherds in the second chapter of Luke. The
shepherds are simply described as 'living out in
the fields' when something supernatural con-
fronts them. It is interesting to note that the
appearance of angels and the heavenly choir took
place while shepherds were in the midst of their
work. They were simply making a living. There
was nothing special or unusual about their job,
nothing out of the ordinary about their activity.

We tend to associate the miraculous with the
spectacular. When God works we expect His
performance to be striking and larger than life.
Only then can we concede that He is really at

work. God is fully capable of doing the spectacular and sometimes does but I believe that He often operates in the realm of the mundane. People in Jesus' time asked for a miraculous sign, but he instead pointed them to the sign of Jonah, which signified the kind of death Christ would experience and the mercy and grace that would follow.

In short, the miraculous is in the monotonous. Notice the contrast, for without the monotony there is nothing miraculous to talk about. It is what makes miracles well, miracles – out of the drab, some incident shines forth, out of dullness, an event bursts out in full colour, out of the ordinary, the extraordinary happens – all cutting through the drudgery of everyday life. And so it was on the morning of 11 December 1998.

I awoke early having just arrived the day before in Yangon, Myanmar, for my third visit. My sleep had been short but deep. Kenneth Bong, the Director of OM Singapore who was sharing the room with me, also rose early. The MV *Doulos* was coming alongside the pier at 7.30 am and we wanted to be there to welcome her. After a quick breakfast we made our way to the pier.

We were not the only ones there to welcome the ship. Several hundred flag-waving school children in their green and white uniforms were already on the jetty. A cultural troupe from the Ministry of Hotels and Tourism, official hosts of the ship visit, was warming up with a Burmese rendition of the popular Spanish song, 'Macarena'. Among the group were eight ladies in stunning traditional tribal costumes. Several smaller groups from some local churches were standing at the end of the pier holding Christian banners.

Everyone was in a festive mood. Everyone that is except *Doulos* representatives Steve Cassidy, Peter Capell, Peter Conlan and a Burmese shipping agent. They had good reason to be apprehensive, this was the first ever visit of the MV *Doulos* to military-ruled Myanmar. No OM ship had ever visited before.

What made this visit to Yangon so special? One Christian leader described the Myanmar church as a hermit church in a hermit nation. According to a local pastor the Myanmar church had been cut off from the international Christian community for more than three decades. This alone made the visit of *Doulos* a significant event.

Never before in history had a Christian ship sailed into Yangon, the heart of a devout Buddhist nation. To be given an official welcome by the government was then nothing short of a miracle, especially knowing the past record of the military government.

It had taken all of 26 years to finally get one of our ships into the country. Various attempts were made to bring an OM ship to Burma, the name Myanmar was formerly known by. Survey trips made in the early 1970s and enquiries made in 1980 failed to result in a *Logos* or *Doulos* visit to Rangoon, now Yangon. Local Christians felt then that a high-profile visit might jeopardise the church's fragile relationship with the authorities.

In 1996 Peter Conlan, who was instrumental in clearing the way for the *Logos* and later the *Doulos*, to visit Shanghai, made a trip to Myanmar to find out if a visit would now be possible. Unlike earlier attempts, the reception he received from the authorities and church leaders was favourable and positive. The view of the local church leaders was that the situation had changed sufficiently to make a *Doulos* visit viable. The Myanmar authorities later confirmed their official invitation for the *Doulos* to visit Yangon in 1998.

In the past last minute complications had resulted in the cancellation of a ship visit to a particular port so we were quite prepared for this possibility. We would only relax when we actually saw the ship in port.

In the ensuing year and a half, Steve Cassidy, leader of the line-up team, would visit Yangon to follow up on the goodwill that Peter had experienced. Each time he reported that the process was going to be tedious and cumbersome, but was going as planned. The process was complex – Steve and Peter Capell had to liaise with the Ministry of Hotels and Tourism, our official host, and the Ministry in turn had to co-ordinate arrangements with 16 other departments!

To allow the meetings to run smoothly, at least in the initial rounds, the absence of foreigners was preferred. Thus a local contact was appointed to represent the *Doulos* line-up team.

Despite the many barriers the team faced there was an overriding sense of faith at work – that the Lord would be able to move mountains and do the impossible for us. But credit must be given to them for their perseverance in working through the process.

A proposed programme was submitted to the government and to our amazement, after some adjustments on both sides, the response was favourable.

The *Doulos* visit was designated a 'Special Project Port', and so those of us living outside the country set about raising the funds needed. As the ship would not be allowed to sell books in Myanmar, the income from which is normally used to meet many of the ship's expenses, sponsorship was sought to cover fuel costs, port fees, line-up expenses and a host of other expenditures.

Several projects for which permission was granted (including a donation of books to educational institutions and provision of some basic materials to orphanages) saw generous donations from ship supporters around the world.

On his list of educational institutions to be given a donation of books Steve had included a short list of theological seminaries. He admitted that he typed in the names of the seminaries to test the water – to see if there was something OM could do to help the Christian colleges. To his surprise permission was granted and several seminaries benefited from the donation of theological books.

'This is historical!' Steve exclaimed. For more than 30 years the importation of Christian books was banned in this country. The dearth of educational books was also quite obvious on looking at the bookstores in town. Most books on sale were photocopied, with blue plastic covers to make them a little more attractive. The *Doulos* was effectively the first vehicle to bring in a consignment of books.

An official programme was also submitted. As the visit was planned for December, the theme of Christmas was proposed. The visit was to last six days and included an Official Reception for the government officials and diplomatic community, receptions for the medical community, the academic fraternity, church representatives, theological students and the business community.

On the Sunday children from several orphanages would be invited to the ship for some approved activities while members of the ship would attend churches and share in the celebration of Christmas. The National Theatre was booked for an international programme called 'Christmas around the world'.

By mid-1998, Steve informed us that the authorities had finally given the green light.

And so there we were, waiting nervously for the *Doulos* to sail up the Irrawaddy River into the heart of Yangon.

'There it is!' someone shouted, pointing at the distant horizon. It was not difficult to recognise the big 'T' mast of the *Doulos*. The river was heavy with traffic – barges, bum-boats, ferries, motor-boats – and so the *Doulos* had to go carefully. As it neared the children started waving their flags and the troupe began singing and dancing. Camera shutters clicked non-stop. Having been briefed earlier by Steve through radio the ship crew was all properly dressed and standing by to return the warm gesture of welcome by the Burmese parties on the pier.

Whereas bigger ships in major ports dwarfed the *Doulos*, in Yangon she was the biggest vessel on the water and looked imposing. Although the ship was filthy (the long voyage from the Maldives had meant water rationing and so no water had been wasted on washing the ship!), she still looked beautiful.

I remember a time in Port Klang, Malaysia, when the ship was berthed next to the Star Cruise's gigantic *Aquarius*. The officers from *Aquarius* were seen streaming down the gangway to board the *Doulos*. Listed in *The Guinness Book of Records* as the world's oldest passenger liner still in operation, and only two years younger than the *Titanic*, *Doulos* is the grand old lady of passenger ships! We were indeed proud of her.

Once alongside, Captain Graham Bird and Director, Lloyd Nicholas, disembarked to greet all onshore. Balloons were released into the air and the programme was launched.

A work team was immediately dispatched to the Agape Orphanage 40 kilometres away. With only six days and a list of jobs to be done we had no time to lose. Another team, much larger, led by ship veteran, Kenny Gan, left the same evening for Mandalay, Myanmar's second largest city, which was several hundred kilometres up river. They took with them a load of books to be donated to several institutions. We later heard from Kenny that things did not go entirely smoothly for them. Due to the lack of communication from Yangon the officials there were not so co-operative. Even after authorisation was given things did not improve but they were still able to fulfil the programme as scheduled.

Several hundred 'Christmas Love Packs' were put together to be given to orphanages in and around Yangon. These contained basics like toothpaste, toothbrush, soapbox, a New Testament, a Christmas storybook, school clothes and a bag – items considered luxuries by the orphans' standards.

The children yelled with delight when *Doulos* teams handed out the packs plus teddy bears of all sizes. Essentials such as rice, medicine, vitamins, ionised salt, mosquito nets and other supplies were also given to the orphanages. One orphanage director told a *Doulos* team leader that they were down to their last one and a half bags of rice when the Christmas gifts came!

The communication from Peter Capell in October summed up our desire to help the orphans

Dr Simon took us to an inner city orphanage housing 60 children. We entered the small compound and were immediately confronted with the very real and pressing needs facing these children. An open sewer streamed within feet of the primitive cooking arrangements, or so-called kitchen! Two outhouses on stilts dumped on open ground a few feet from the house. They can't serve their meals without stepping over a trough of raw reeking sewage. No running water was available. Water had to be hauled from the deep well. The pitifully small ground was a soggy mixture of water and sludge, interspersed with buildings that housed the children in very cramped bedrooms. There is little room to play except for the street. The need was overwhelming! I could feel tears welling up in my eyes.

Years of bloody civil war, poverty and hunger have produced a forgotten generation of orphans. Abandoned by their families and unwanted by society, stories of children being taken over the border and sold into Thailand's sleazy sex trade are sadly too common. Yet these orphans are beautiful children living often in very brutal circumstances. Many end up on the streets or in Buddhist temples.

The Official Reception was scheduled for the first evening. The night before Peter Conlan pulled me to one side to tell me that two days earlier the United Nations had celebrated the fiftieth anniversary of Human Rights. In Yangon a meeting had been organised but no one from the cabinet attended. 'Tonight,' Peter said, 'Secretary One, the most powerful man in the country, and all his cabinet ministers, are coming to the Official Reception.' If the press, especially the foreign press, got hold of this information and made it known outside of the country, the *Doulos* might well be caught in the middle of a controversial situation – something we wanted to avoid. At such a late stage there really was nothing we, as human beings, could do.

My response to Peter did not surprise him. I said that the exact schedule of the ship, as we both knew, had been confirmed several weeks earlier, and there was no way we could have known about the Human Rights day that fell just two days before our arrival. Furthermore, I was convinced of God's timing. After all, we had taken 26 years to get here! I continued in my un-accustomed confidence, 'This project all along has been a matter of faith, and we just have to trust the Lord to work this out for us.'

The Official Reception was well attended. I met with the Thai, Laotian and the Egyptian ambassadors. The Thai Ambassador, like most of the other guests, asked many questions about the ship. The Secretary One arrived promptly and was hosted in the VIP lounge on the ship. The Director, Captain and Peter entertained him and took him to the book exhibition. A national television crew was there to ensure every minute of this occasion was recorded.

Later Peter announced to the reception that due to an on-coming fever, the Secretary One had asked to be excused and left the ship, but not before issuing an invitation to the *Doulos* to return next year. With such an endorsement the next few days proved to be rather smooth sailing.

Several customs officers were based on board to monitor the ship and sometimes ship personnel were searched. The officers were all quite friendly though.

On Saturday, having just returned to the ship from the city, I answered a call for help to offload boxes of books for the institutions. Together with several of the ship crew I joined in the human chain formed to move hundreds of boxes of books from the book-hold up to the deck, and then to send them tumbling down the conveyor belt on the gangway to the quayside. It was tiring work, but we were all motivated by the fact that we were creating history with this consignment.

Each institution was given an average of 35 boxes of books. The consignment for the universities included a set of encyclopaedia, medical books, English books, dictionaries and an assortment of different titles. As for the theological seminaries, we packed Bible commentaries, study Bibles, theological volumes and a variety of Christian books. We watched with immense satisfaction as the various groups from the institutions collected their books. I had never seen happier faces. One university, I learned, only had 100 US dollars available for the purchase of books for their library. Our donation far exceeded their budget!

In total the ship donated one thousand books to the National Library, and six hundred each to 15 university libraries, 50 books to each of Myanmar's 52 district libraries, with a set of encyclopaedia for each. The book donation not only met an important need; it helped to build friendship and paved the way for the ship to visit in the first place.

'Christmas Around the World' was billed as the Saturday night main event on the ship, and I suspected, in Yangon. Almost the entire ship family turned up to support the event. More than a thousand guests were already seated when an announcement was made requesting the *Doulos* crew to give up their seats to the Burmese ticket holders. It was an enjoyable night for the many that came.

On the Sunday several hundred orphans were greeted and entertained by the team of *Doulos* clowns. This, and other things the ship crew did, was our way of expressing the love of Christ. On the same day, 110 *Doulos* team members were allowed unlimited freedom to share their music and testimonies in 32 churches in Yangon. In the history of the *Doulos* there have been few Sundays like it. For the Christian community of Myanmar there had not been a Sunday like this in more than 30 years!

One typical comment came from a local pastor, 'It is so wonderful to have the ship visit Yangon. You have brought us great encouragement!' Teddy, our Burmese representative, informed us that the local pastors were encouraged to see the leaders from the ship speaking in their churches as well as in their work clothes sweating it out on the ship.

I was part of a team of five from the *Doulos* ministering in a charismatic church situated in the centre of the city, four floors up in an old building. Some parts of Yangon reminded me of Calcutta with its colonial influence in the architecture. It also reminded me of Singapore in the early 1960s where I grew up.

Before we started the Burmese pastor reminded us to refrain from saying anything political or against another religion in our presentation. 'O yes,' he continued, 'please do not stamp your feet when you sing.' The pastor explained that this request was due to complaints from people downstairs!

The Burmese Christians could certainly sing! They had great natural musical talent – the musicians played by ear and the youth choir simply blended in harmony. Our team introduced themselves – one shared her testimony and two sang. One girl did a mime and I preached. As it was nearly Christmas, I delivered a Christmas message. By the time I finished I was drenched in perspiration – the hall was packed to capacity with three hundred people and only several fans to give relief from the heat. I felt downhearted; convinced I had made a bad job of preaching that morning.

To my surprise the pastor, sensing that I had just given an evangelistic message, gave an invitation in the Burmese language for people to receive the Christ of Christmas. About twenty people promptly stood up in response to this call. I concluded that the pastor was better at persuading than I was at preaching!

That night it was the turn of the medical community to have their reception. My good friend, Dr Goh Wei Leong, also visiting the ship, was involved in the reception. He told me that everyone spoke English, they were the elite of the community. One doctor went up to the book exhibition afterwards and was heard to exclaim, 'All these I see I can only dream about!' A frequently heard comment by then was – 'We hope you are able to sell books next time!'

In the course of the evening one man admitted to Wei Leong that he was not a doctor, but an engineer. He confessed that he managed to sneak in with the crowd. The following day, he was at the foot of the gangway. Wei Leong met him again. He said, 'When I read about the ship in the newspapers, I told myself that no matter what, I must come and see it. And seeing the ship is the highlight of my year!'

Despite the fact that all who accepted our invitation to the receptions on board had to have their names submitted to the authorities no one seemed to mind. Attendance was an almost perfect one hundred per cent.

Being the most senior OM leader present I was given the responsibility of addressing the reception for the church representatives. The thought of addressing such an august group would normally have given me the jitters, but for some inexplicable reason, I was actually looking forward to it.

Myanmar has the biggest Protestant church between India and China numbering 1.5 million Christians, mostly Baptists and mostly tribal. What could I say to their church leaders that they had not heard already? I prepared a simple message that I prayed would minister and encourage the group gathered – I had been told that this was the purpose of the reception.

I peeped into the lounge and saw that it was full, everyone invited had turned up – heads of major church denominations, heads of various Christian councils, senior pastors, heads of different organisations, Christian and church leaders, anyone who was anybody in the Christian community (i.e. all the heavyweights!) were present. What was so amazing about this gathering was that never before in recent history had a group like this met under one roof. The *Doulos* had achieved something quite unique.

The Lord must have settled my nerves as I walked towards the lectern. I began by offering to answer any questions the audience might have. The first question would normally have rattled me, but I was well prepared. 'In what capacity are you addressing us?' someone asked. Whether this was asked out of curiosity or out of rudeness I was not sure. Knowing the politeness of the Burmese, I believe it was out of curiosity. I told them that I was the Regional Consultant of the ship ministry and this reply seemed to satisfy them.

'I am here to encourage you,' I began. A Burmese pastor interpreted my message although many that were older would understand English. I spoke on an uncontroversial subject – 'Four lessons from an old ship'. How could a ship as old as the *Doulos* manage to survive two world wars and outlive other younger and newer ships? What were the qualities she possessed that had given her such an enduring life?

I shared with them four things:

1. The ability to change – the ship had had no less than four re-fits and changes of purpose.

2. The ability to face adversities – during our tenure she had faced several attacks in different forms.

3. Knowing her limitations – after all she was no longer young!

4. Old ship, young people – the average age of the crew was between 20 and 40 years.

Applying these principles to Christian leadership was simple and straightforward. The Lord had given me these thoughts earlier as I was thinking about what to say to them. I remembered to stay out of politics and religion!

After the reception, several came up to thank me for the word I shared. Seeing them there and the smiles on their faces was encouragement itself.

Throughout the six days the Ministry of Hotels and Tourism organised group tours for the crew.

The *Doulos* crew was introduced to the rich
Burmese culture and religion. A visit to a pagoda
was a must on these tours. Due to the favourable
exchange rate the small amount of pocket money
stretched a long way for the crew!

Of the orphanages we were involved with
none received as much attention as the Agape
Orphanage. All the children there were under-
nourished and lacking in the most basic health
and material care. Each day groups from the ship
would travel to the orphanage; this was an hour's
journey. Their job was to plant fruit trees so that
the children could have a long-term supply of
fruit – lack of vitamins was the cause of many of
the skin problems suffered by the children.

When we got there on the fifth day the work
team from the *Doulos* had already finished
building the concrete latrines, a concrete water
tank and a host of other practical jobs. Some men
were still drilling a pipe into the ground to get
water; they were halfway towards the four
hundred-foot depth. We were also able to
bring with us some basic medication for the
orphanage's use. By the time the ship left many
friendships had been forged between the *Doulos*
crew and the orphans.

Friendships were also made between the ship
crew and many Burmese Christians. As the ship
sailed away, we were very aware that the Lord,
in the six days of the programme and the months
beforehand, had been able to do exceedingly

abundantly beyond our expectation. It was a miracle only God could perform through the hard work of faithful men like Steve, Peter Capell, Peter Conlan, all on board and a team of volunteers and advisors.

I must not forget Teddy and Helen (not their real names), a young couple who continue to live in Myanmar to represent us. It was while serving on board the *Doulos* nine years previously that Teddy had prayed a simple prayer to God – 'God, please bring *Doulos* to my country'.

Chapter Sixteen

Travel Tales

*'The Lord will keep you from all harm – he
will watch over your life; the Lord will watch
over your coming and going both now and
forevermore.'*
Psalm 121:7–8

Some things are unforgettable. Do you remember
the first trip you took overseas? Most people will.

'What is it like travelling the way you do?' is a
question I am often asked. If I am going to a new
place for the first time I am usually excited and
prepare by reading about the place to be visited.
However, having travelled now for so many
years, there are not many places left that I have
not visited. In most cases I am returning to the
same place for perhaps the umpteenth time. The
novelty has worn off.

To cope with this I use a simple strategy –
which is to learn at least one thing that I didn't
know before and to observe more keenly an

aspect of human behaviour that I might have otherwise missed. Whereas in the past I used to just work with little or no rest, nowadays I make time for some recreation, even if it is just for a very short period.

The following tales are just some I have collected in recent years of travel.

No Man's Land

No Man's Land is the space between two countries or the land found between the immigration checkpoints of two countries. The No Man's Land between India and Bangladesh was about one hundred metres wide when we crossed it in 1976.

We entered Bangladesh in our vehicle using an International Vehicle Carnet, like a vehicle passport. After spending one month in Bangladesh we made our way back to the border to re-enter India in order to take the MV *Chidambaram* from Madras to Malaysia.

At the border our vehicle was refused re-entry to India. Apparently in the month we were in Bangladesh the Indian transport authority had invalidated the International Vehicle Carnet. John, our driver, was dispatched to Calcutta to sort this problem out, leaving Frankie and I to guard the van in No Man's Land. John eventually returned seven days later! We were left stranded with no way of knowing what was happening (we found out later that John had suffered from diarrhoea for two days).

John had left us with enough money for only two days. When our money ran out we explained our predicament and negotiated an arrangement with the 'chai' shop to provide us with meals three times a day on credit until John returned. Amazingly, the 'chai wallah' agreed to it. With our meals taken care of, we went in search of somewhere to wash. We found a communal tap outside a village not far from our van.

To kill time we played Frisbee with the village kids, which turned out to be a great hit. Frankie and I also spent a lot of time praying and reading. I had a great time listening to music, messages on cassettes and simply worshipping the Lord.

Trucks from India off-loading their goods onto trucks from Bangladesh, and vice versa, also used the No Man's Land. Sacks of grain, rice, sugar, flour, etc, were imported and exported this way.

One morning Frankie and I were awoken by a loud crash. The sideboard of a truck parked alongside us had given way and smashed our side window, completely destroying it. It was then that John appeared out of nowhere. Without hesitation he demanded 500 Rupees from the driver, this was an exorbitant amount but John was not in an accommodative mood after a bout of diarrhoea and frustration. After some haggling we settled for 250 Rupees, still a lot by Indian standards. It more than paid for the five days of food for us!

John had been able to validate the carnet and we were only too eager to get out of the No Man's Land. On arrival at the West Bengal OM base outside of Calcutta Allan Witt, a mechanic, bought a piece of glass, cut it, and promptly mounted it onto the damaged area. Allan used the 50 Rupees left from the compensation to pay for the glass and charged us nothing for the repair. Our seven days in No Man's Land had cost us nothing except for time lost!

No-Frills Travel

An appointment was made for me to meet with the Regional Superintendent of another organisation to discuss co-operation in a particular programme of common interest. The representatives from Malaysia would drive to South Thailand and I was to make my own way and meet up with them in a city called Pattani.

I left home at 5.30 am taking a taxi to the airport in time to catch the first flight to Kuala Lumpur. I was just in time to make the connection to Kota Baru via an hour stopover in Alor Star. Once in Kota Baru I took a taxi to the town centre in order to catch the border-taxi. The border between Malaysia and Thailand was separated by a river, which happened to be in No Man's Land. I took the ferry across to Takbai, the Thai border town. There was no bus running as it was a public holiday and so I had to take yet another taxi ride to Narathiwat.

Upon arrival in Narathiwat I phoned Don, my host, only to be told by his Thai servant that he was in another town an hour away. For the next two hours I tried, unsuccessfully, to contact him. I was stranded. I strolled up and down the main road wondering what to do next. Then I told the Lord that I was stranded and asked Him if he could help me to somehow make some connection with the people I was supposed to meet. Soon afterwards along came the van carrying the Malaysian brothers I was to rendezvous with! Together we travelled another hour and a half to Pattani. We arrived 5.00 pm Thai time.

After keeping the appointment the following morning, I made my way back to Singapore, reversing the entire process.

I share this story in defence of people who travel regularly. Some non-travellers tend to believe that travelling must be fun. I want them to see that it also involves hard work.

Rock and Roll Love Boat?

In August 1995 I sailed on the MV *Doulos* from Durban to Port Elizabeth, South Africa. It was a two-day voyage and I thought that while at sea, without a busy programme, I could get a lot of work done. I was mistaken.

Before departure the Captain gave instructions to lash down everything on deck and below deck in preparation for a rough voyage ahead. The following morning when I awoke the ship was rolling sideways and bouncing bow and aft. I went up to the bridge to find out what was happening. The forecastle was now out of bounds to all personnel as 30-feet waves were pouring in. Graham Bird, the Chief Officer, who was later to become the *Doulos* Captain, informed me that there were cross-currents near the Cape of Good Hope, between the Atlantic and the Indian Oceans. The ship was forced to reduce her speed by half and so our arrival was delayed.

I descended to the deck below, and found half the ship family flat on their backs with seasickness. The seasick were watching video after video in an attempt to take their minds off the motion of the ship. Thankfully I continue to be a good sailor!

The Ultimate in Air Travel

Not long ago I enjoyed the ultimate in air travel. Travelling on an off-peak special offer with Singapore Airlines in a 747 MegaTop I had four seats all to myself on a half-empty flight to London.

The individualised audiovisual entertainment had 21 channels to choose from, 12 movies in English, Chinese and French, plus channels on news, sports, flight path, and ten Nintendo games. My only complaint was I didn't have enough time to enjoy it all – the flight was too short!

The flip side of the hand-held remote control was a telephone that could be used to call any seats on the aircraft or any part of the world. I simply couldn't resist the temptation to call Justin, my son, to tell him that I was thirty thousand feet in the air above the Himalayan Mountains.

The return trip was just as enjoyable. Several years down the line Singapore Airlines has just launched into a new generation of inflight service. Recently I was thrilled to fly on the first upgraded MegaTop plane!

An Angel in the Air

I cannot remember his name or what he looked like, but I do know that he was an angel, or close to one.

On my way to Turkmenistan to attend the funeral of Byoung Soo, I struck up a conversation with an air steward on the flight. He was surprised to learn that I was going to Ashgabad for a funeral. He didn't know where Ashgabad was, and I painted to him a very grim picture of the place. He felt sorry for me. When I disembarked he wished me a good trip.

Five days later, having attended the funeral and spent time with those affected by the death of the Korean brother, I flew from Ashgabad to Istanbul to take the connection back to Singapore. At Istanbul I bumped into the same steward. We exchanged pleasantries and discovered that we would be on the same flight again.

It is my custom to buy something, usually a toy, for my children when I am on a trip. Friends and my wife, in particular, chide me against such unnecessary spending but I think that what I spend on these gifts is actually far less than what I spend taking the children on outings when I am home. I had been away the week before in Papua New Guinea, only to rush off the following day to Turkmenistan, so I was anxious to get them something. I had looked for something suitable at both Ashgabad and Istanbul airports but had been unsuccessful in my search.

As soon as I was seated on the plane the steward, who was not assigned to my cabin section on this flight, gave me a bag of airline goodies. He said, 'For your kids' and left. I didn't see him again. Inside the bag were building bricks, jigsaws, a soft toy, souvenir cards, a model plane, and other collectibles. Now I had something to take home!

I always treasure incidents like this when the Lord, sometimes even without prayer, meets the desires of my heart. I believe He can meet yours too.

A Chinese Habit

I lived in Hong Kong from 1990 to 1994. The stereotyping in their movies of their Chinese compatriots across the border was something that amused me. The Chinese man sports a perpetually unkempt and uncombed look. His shirt, normally white in colour, is left hanging out. It is fashionable to wear a blood red or bright orange vest underneath it. If he is sophisticated he will be talking non-stop into his mobile telephone, more often than not he is found squatting at a roadside curb. It is amazing how many things he can do at a time – talking on the telephone, smoking a cigarette, and spitting!

If you plan to travel in China watch out for the spitters. Anticipate them if they are walking towards you, or keep a discreet distance when walking behind them. You just don't know when they will strike, or spit.

This national habit is an art form. First you need to build things up at your throat, mouth and nose. Next comes the clearing of your throat as a warning to those in close proximity. Then you spit. Women enjoy equality in this national habit. Who said China is a land of restrictions? In this there is none – you can do it on roads, buses, trains, in airports and on aeroplanes. You are even allowed to do it in front of high officials simply because officials engage in it as well.

All Chinese are Doctors

If you don't believe me just tell your Chinese friend or friends the next time you are sick. What they do for a job does not matter. Diagnosis is free; your illness will be exactly the same as what they suffered recently. The prescription is guaranteed, because so-and-so ate the same thing and look how healthy he or she is now. The prescription is normally a combination of all kinds of roots, herbs and foods. Eating something is a solution to all illnesses, including diarrhoea and nausea. You must eat to get well.

Chinese medicine boasts of cures for all kinds of ailments. I wondered while visiting China if some remedy could be found for a receding hairline. Plucking up courage I marched up to the pharmaceutical counter of a large store not realising that there is no such thing as a private consultation.

I explained my problem to the woman behind the counter and asked if she had a solution. She recommended one particular brand and then took two minutes to broadcast in a loud voice all the problems that she was convinced I had. A small crowd of on-lookers gathered to listen – men and women all with full heads of hair. By now everybody in the store knew about my problem. I asked the sales assistant to lower her voice, as I could not handle the attention my hair was receiving. It was then her turn to blush!

You Look Christian!

I have always wondered what a Christian should look like. I remember the first time I walked into a church – I had accepted the Lord the week before and did not know what to expect. A well-intentioned friend had told me that I must not wear slippers to church. Several months later, I was told to cut my hair. Later I was told not to wear jeans to church. Since then I have attended churches in many countries and I am not sure if there is a standard way that a Christian should look.

I remember an occasion when, Wei Leong, a good friend and travelling companion, and I were returning from a week of consultation in Hyderabad, India. It had been a fruitful visit. We boarded the plane bound for Singapore in Madras and took our seats. A male passenger was already seated in the aisle seat. No sooner had we sat down than he asked 'Are you Christians?' 'Yes, we are.' I replied.

Wei Leong and I were a little taken aback by this very direct line of questioning. But we introduced ourselves. He was from Singapore and a businessman. Our conversation continued, 'What makes you think we are Christians?' I asked Mr Tan (not his real name). 'Well, it is the way you look and behave,' he affirmed.

Mr Tan said he did go to church now and then. When asked what he thought of Jesus Christ his answer was as unexpected as it was emotional. He said that every time he looked at the cross and pondered on why a man would die for the sins of humankind, he would become distressed and tears would well up uncontrollably. As if to prove this point, the tears started flowing down his cheeks as he was speaking. Wei Leong and I watched in amazement at his display of un-ashamed emotion.

We continued our conversation. He asked more questions about the Bible and I did the best I could to answer them. I realised our plane was fast approaching Changi Airport, Singapore. I explained to him in as clear a way as I could, the need to have his sins cleansed and his life given to Jesus. He assured me that he understood the Gospel but he was not ready. I finally left it at that and did not push him.

As we left the plane, Wei Leong remarked, 'That's the most amazing encounter I have ever had. He sounded so ready.' As we have sown we pray that others might get to reap the harvest of this particular man.

Chapter Seventeen

Navel-gazing

*'Do nothing out of selfish ambition or vain
conceit, but in humility consider others better
than yourselves. Each of you should look not only
to your own interests, but also to
the interests of others.'*
Philippians 2:3–4

Navel-gazing is a strange habit and yet all of us
have a tendency to engage in it. The ideal position
for navel-gazing is sitting down. It is the most
comfortable position and requires only a little
effort and energy, but affords one the best view.
From such a position one can stare for long
periods. It is possible to get emotional and upset
about what one sees if one stares long enough. It
is not difficult in due course to empathise with
what one is looking at.

Let me warn you however of the hazards
associated with this peculiar occupation. When
you engage in it long enough your vision

becomes unreliable and when you venture from your sitting position chances are you will lose your balance and injure yourself in a fall. The world around you becomes unreal. My advice to you is to remain where you are, but even this is risky, for I can guarantee that you will be resigned to a state of inertia, apathy, or even worse, paralysis.

Navel-gazing is a preoccupation with something small magnified out of all proportion. A small thing becomes a big problem.

What am I trying to say? I want to sound a warning to Christians. It is possible that when we are absorbed in *self* – self-examination, self-study, self-consciousness, self-preservation, self-interest and self-pity – we forget that there are others and that there is a world out there. Please do not misunderstand me, a certain measure of loving self is healthy, after all, the Bible tells us to 'love your neighbour as you love yourself' (Lev. 19:18). But when we become overly absorbed with self, that's when the danger begins. The Bible teaches us to be alert and aware of others. Christianity is about others.

As I come to the end of this book, I hope I have given you a glimpse of how colourful our world is. I trust you will have grasped that the world out there is ready for us – a world hungering and thirsting for the true answer which is found only in Jesus Christ.

We have Him. Now He wants others to have Him as well. And I believe He wants you to make this known to them.

Will you?

Chapter Eighteen

Epilogue

Seven months have passed since I started writing this book. To be honest I did not expect the book to take the form it has. What began as tentative became increasingly substantive as I continued probing into the recesses of my mind calling up memories and lessons learned through the years I have spent serving the Lord. What I have written is by no means comprehensive but I do trust that in its pages you have found encouragement.

I began with the intention of driving home the fact that God uses all kinds of people – including the average! I see myself as an average person; everything that I am and do, education, sports, swimming, running, music, communication ability, preaching, is average. If you like me are an average person, there is cause for hope and promise. This doesn't mean you will tread the exact path I have trod – your path may prove to be even more meaningful and profitable.

As I have read and re-read my manuscript, I have become acutely aware that 'tentative' and 'average' are the two words that probably best describe my life experiences.

You may have noticed that this book also captures the story of OM in its developmental years in East Asia and the Pacific. I don't think you will find it difficult to understand why OM is a movement I love and believe in. I love it not so much for its professionalism – although it has a high degree of that – as for its open-armed approach to the average, the tentative, the not one hundred per cent sure if missions is their life's cup of tea Christian who wants to live out his or her commitment in missions.

Like OM in East Asia Pacific, I will, God willing, continue to learn as I mature in the entire mission enterprise of involving the church and individuals in fulfilling the purposes of God.

Been there, done that and God is still not done with me yet.

Distinctives

Vaughan Roberts

ISBN 1–85078–331–4

In a fresh and readable style, the author of *Turning Points*, Vaughan Roberts, issues a challenging call to Christians to live out their faith. We should be different from the world around us – Christian distinctives should set us apart in how we live, think, act and speak. Targeting difficult but crucial areas such as our attitude to money and possessions, sexuality, contentment, relativism and service, this is holiness in the tradition of J.C. Ryle for the contemporary generation.

VAUGHAN ROBERTS is rector of St Ebbe's Church, Oxford. He is a popular conference speaker and University Christian Union speaker.

OM
publishing

Operation World
Pray for the World

Patrick Johnstone

ISBN 1–85078–120–6

The definitive guide to praying effectively and specifically for every country of the world, formatted for daily use, or to dip into when praying for missionaries or around current events. Using this book is an excellent way to involve yourself in global mission.

Stop, Check, Go

Ditch Townsend

ISBN 1–85078–364–0

Anyone planning on going overseas on a short-term missions trip should soak up the contents of this invaluable book. Helping them to prepare practically, personally and spiritually, this superb book will ensure that the benefits of the experience are greatly increased to all concerned.

OM
publishing

Out of the Comfort Zone

GEORGE VERWER

ISBN 1–85078–353–5

Reading this book could seriously change your attitude!
George Verwer has managed to write a book that is humble
and hard-hitting at the same time. He doesn't pull any
punches in his heart's cry for a 'grace-awakened' approach
to mission, and wants to cut through superficial
'spirituality' that may be lurking inside you. George Verwer
is known throughout the world as a motivator and
mobiliser. *Out of the Comfort Zone* should only be read by
those who are willing to accept God's grace, catch His vision
and respond with action in the world of mission.

OM
publishing

The George Verwer Collection

ISBN 1–85078–296–2

George Verwer has inspired and encouraged thousands in their Christian discipleship. Now three of his best-loved books, *The Revolution of Love*, *No Turning Back* and *Hunger For Reality* are brought together in this three-in-one collection. The trilogy points us to love as the central theme of Christian life, calls us to effective service and revolutionizes our lives so that they are consistent and productive.

'Immensely readable and full of the practical aspects of spiritual principles.'

Evangelism Today

'A wealth of good material.'

Martin Goldsmith
Church of England Newspaper

Over 100,000 copies sold.

GEORGE VERWER is the founder and International Director of Operation Mobilisation. He has an international preaching ministry based in Britain.

OM
publishing

Serving as Senders

Neal Pirolo

ISBN 1–85078–199–0

'This key book makes the point that mobilizers – the senders – are as crucial to the cause of missions as frontline missionaries. It is a book just crammed with solid, exciting insights on the most hurting link in today's mission movement.'

Ralph Winter
U.S. Center for World Mission

'Unless the Church and God's people respond to this book's message, the work of reaching the unreached is going to be greatly hindered. Every committed sender needs to get involved in distributing this book.'

George Verwer
Operation Mobilisation

NEAL PIROLO is the founding Director of Emmaus Road International, San Diego, California, mobilizing churches, training cross-cultural teams, and networking fellowships with national ministries around the world.

OM
publishing

Future Leader

Viv Thomas

ISBN 0–85364–949–9

Leadership is a key to success in any organisation.

All the more reason to get it right, says Viv Thomas in a book that sets out to discern the kind of leadership that is needed as we enter a new millennium.

Drawing on biblical models and organisational management research, along with personal experience of some of the evangelical world's most influential leaders, the author provides a model of leadership that is:

- Driven by compassion, not obsession.
- Rooted in relationships, not systems.
- Promotes life, not self-image.

If we fail in these areas, he argues, most of what we do in terms of goals, strategies, skills, mission and communication will eventually be blown away.

This stimulating and inspiring book will test all who might aspire to lead.

VIV THOMAS is the International Co-ordinator of Leadership Development with Operation Mobilisation. He has a world-wide preaching and teaching ministry, with an emphasis on developing leaders. He is also a visiting lecturer at All Nations Christian College in Hertfordshire.

paternoster
press